TALES OF REAL
SURVIVAL

Paul Dowswell

Designed by Nigel Reece

Additional design by Fiona Brown

Illustrated by Ian Jackson, Sean Wilkinson,
Janos Marffy and Guy Smith

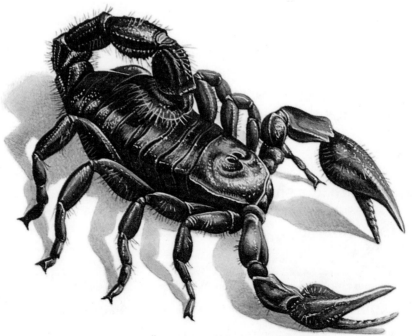

SCHOLASTIC INC.
New York Toronto London Auckland Sydney
Mexico City New Delhi Hong Kong Buenos Aires

Contents

Survival essentials

The stories in this book are about people who stared death in the face and lived to tell the tale. Many of them – explorers, military personnel, mountaineers – were already in extraordinary circumstances when disaster struck. But others – passengers, workmen, tourists – suddenly found themselves quite unexpectedly fighting for their lives.

Good and bad fortune

What separates the living from the dead when catastrophe strikes? Often it is simply a matter of chance – for example, those on the deck of a sinking ship have a greater chance of escape than their shipmates below. But once the immediate danger has passed, sheer determination can become the most important element in the struggle for survival.

The crew of *Apollo 13* survived a catastrophic explosion on the way to the Moon because they kept cool heads in appalling conditions. Every single one of explorer Ernest Shackleton's Antarctic expedition returned home from the icy polar wastes, because their leader was determined to get them all back alive.

Useful skills

Certainly, expertise can be useful. Paramedic Eric Larsen survived his tussle with a shark because he told rescuers what to do to stop him from bleeding to death, but the key to successful survival seems to be the sheer will to live. You can read about these dramatic stories, and other exciting accounts, in the following pages of Tales of Real Survival.

Dive to disaster

Lieutenant Oliver Naquin, 35, stood face to the wind and spray, on the conning tower of his submarine *Squalus**.

Squalus was brand new and undergoing sea trials before she joined the US Navy as an operational submarine. Now, at 8:40am, on May 23, 1939, she was to carry out a practice crash-dive – an emergency procedure where a submarine under attack on the surface submerges as quickly as possible.

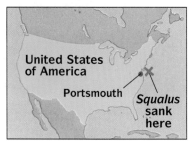

The site of the *Squalus* disaster.

Crash-dive

Naquin ordered his radio operator to report their Atlantic Ocean location to the submarine's home port of Portsmouth, New Hampshire, USA. Then, satisfied that all was well, he hit a button on the bridge which sounded the crash-dive alarm, and hurried below to the control room, closing upper and lower tower hatches as he climbed down.

Inside the submarine a klaxon alarm reverberated around the narrow vessel and men stood alert by dials and instruments, immersed in an intricate sequence of commands. "Secure all vents. Rig sub for diving. Flood main ballast tanks one and two. Open valves – bow buoyancy tanks. Main tanks three to seven – stand by."

Beside Naquin was chief officer Lieutenant Walter Doyle, eyes glued to an instrument

panel known as the "Christmas tree". As all outside vents and hatches were closed, a set of indicator lights changed from red to green, showing that the ship was sealed against the sea.

As the ship's ballast tanks filled with water, *Squalus* swiftly sank to 15m (50ft). Less than a minute after the alarm had sounded, it was as if she had never been there at all.

Flood

As *Squalus* settled underwater, Naquin and Doyle congratulated themselves on a successful operation. But then a fluttering in Naquin's ears caused him to startle, and he knew immediately that something terrible was happening to his ship.

Inside an American submarine much like *Squalus*, a crewman stands beside the diving controls. The "Christmas tree" instrument panel, which indicates whether or not the vessel is sealed for diving, is immediately in front of him.

Lieutenant Oliver Naquin.

An instant later, a wide-eyed sailor looked up from an intercom and shouted that the engine room was flooding. Naquin ordered his craft to come up immediately. Compressed air hissed into the flooded ballast tanks and the stricken submarine began to rise. Although *Squalus*'s bow broke surface, tons of water were now cascading into the rear of the vessel. The weight dragged her stern down sharply and she was swallowed by the sea.

Undersea chaos

Inside was mayhem. In flickering light, tools, fittings, plates and forks, even torpedoes unhinged by the steep angle, rained down on hapless sailors as they tumbled along the ship and into the bulkheads that separated each compartment. In the flooding rear section, soaking men struggled to escape before heavy steel doors were slammed to block off the rising torrent, but many were overwhelmed by the deluge.

Sea water entered the network of interconnecting pipes that

* Squalus (pronounced Skway-lus) is a Latin word meaning "shark".

ran throughout the submarine, and jets of water spurted over men and equipment from bow to stern. Oliver Naquin could only pray that when they hit the bottom his ship would not split open like a bursting balloon.

Battery bomb

But as *Squalus* sank, an equally disastrous fate threatened to overwhelm her. In the forward battery room, ranks of batteries which powered the vessel when she was underwater, were threatening to explode and blow the submarine to fragments.

Acrid blue sheets of flame and spitting white arcs of electricity crackled from terminal to terminal. With extraordinary courage, Chief electrician Lawrence Gainor thrust his arm into the guts of this electronic machinery and shut off the power supply, plunging the submarine into a terrifying darkness.

Four minutes passed before *Squalus* hit the bottom with a jarring thud. But the hull held firm. Several flashlights had been brought to use, and small cones of light now pierced the pitch darkness. Those still left alive began to appraise their situation. Water had entered via an open air vent to the engine room. The "Christmas tree" had indicated that all vents were closed to the sea, so a fault must have developed within this equipment.

In the ghostly glow of a flashlight, crewman Charles Kuney, who manned the intercom connecting all sections to the control room, tried to contact each separate compartment. His calls to the rear of the ship met only with ominous silence.

It soon became clear that all sections behind the control room were now flooded and 26 men there

75 days without a bath

Conditions on board submarines such as *Squalus* were very basic. Men slept in bunks next to torpedoes or among the machinery of the engine room. Although *Squalus* could spend 75 days at sea, there were no showers or laundry facilities for the 56 crew. Some submarines did not have a lavatory and the crew had to use a bucket.

had been trapped and drowned. In the forward section 33 men remained alive, some bruised or bleeding, but none seriously injured. They were 73m (240ft) below the surface.

Naquin knew their only option was to wait for help, although no submariners had been rescued from this depth before.

When she hit the sea bottom *Squalus*'s depth gauge read 73m (240ft).

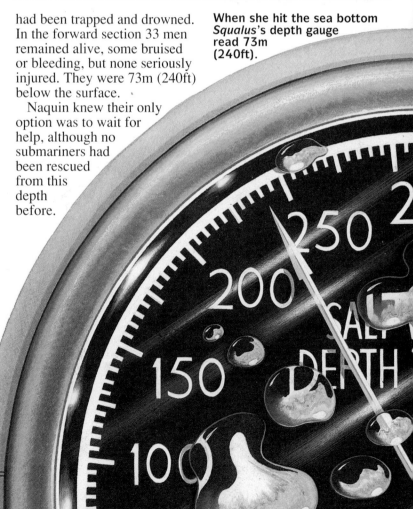

Squalus was due to surface around 9:40am and radio a report to her home base. When no report came, a rescue operation would begin. Meantime, *Squalus* began sending up emergency flares, which floated to the surface and then launched themselves into the air. A marker buoy was also sent up from the submarine, with a telephone link to enable any rescuers to communicate with the submarine's crew. It carried a sign saying

Submarine sunk here.
Telephone inside.

Having survived so far, the biggest threat to the lives of the crew was now suffocation. Not only did they need a supply of air to breathe, they had to ensure they were not asphyxiated by poisonous carbon dioxide, produced by every exhaled breath.

The ship's batteries presented another grave danger. Chemicals within them could react with sea water to produce deadly chlorine gas.

To conserve their air supply, Naquin ordered his men to remain as inactive as possible, with no talking or moving around unless absolutely necessary. Soda lime, a powder which absorbs carbon dioxide,

was scattered around and the men curled up in corners, scarcely illuminated by the one or two lamps that now lit the interior, and waited.

Extra air

All hands were issued with a Momsen Lung. This was a crude form of aqualung which resembled a rubber hot-water bottle attached to a breathing mask. The idea was to give a sailor enough air to breathe while he tried to swim from the submarine escape hatch to the surface. *Squalus* was probably too deep for these devices to work effectively, but they could be of momentary use to the men if the air inside the vessel became too foul to breathe.

Momsen rescue

On shore, *Squalus's* failure to contact her home base had been noted and a rescue operation was gathering momentum. By 1:00pm, underwater rescue expert Charles Momsen (the inventor of the Momsen lung) and a team of divers, had been summoned up from Washington. *Squalus's*

Charles Momsen.

sister ship *Sculpin* and several tugs were all dispatched to the site to assist in the rescue. In New London, 320km (200 miles) south of Portsmouth, the US Navy rescue vessel *Falcon* prepared to join them. *Falcon* carried a McCann Rescue Chamber – a newly invented diving bell based on an idea of Momsen's. This had never been used in a real-life rescue before and training exercises had been at shallower depths, but without the chamber any rescue would be impossible.

Sculpin arrives

At 2:00pm, after a five-hour wait, the crew of *Squalus* heard the dull drubbing of propeller blades above their ship. The *Sculpin* had arrived. Contact was quickly established via the telephone in the marker buoy.

Sculpin's captain took details of the depth and location of the sunken submarine but, before any more could be said, the line snapped, cutting *Squalus*

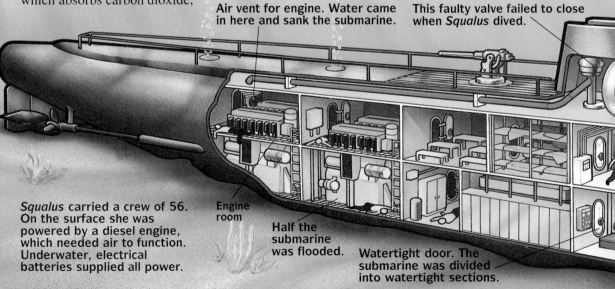

Air vent for engine. Water came in here and sank the submarine.

This faulty valve failed to close when *Squalus* dived.

Squalus carried a crew of 56. On the surface she was powered by a diesel engine, which needed air to function. Underwater, electrical batteries supplied all power.

Engine room

Half the submarine was flooded.

Watertight door. The submarine was divided into watertight sections.

off from the outside world. It was 7:30pm that evening before the rescuers located her again, when the tug *Penacook*, after trawling for four hours, hooked a grapple onto a railing on *Squalus*'s deck.

Aboard the submarine the temperature had dropped to 4°C (39°F) and dank, dripping condensation filled the already waterlogged interior. Naquin ordered blankets to be distributed to his weary crew, waiting silently in the dark. The stale air though, made them drowsy and, despite their fear and cold, many whiled away the waiting hours in an uneasy half-sleep.

Above, another tug, *Wandank*, had arrived and was attempting to make contact with *Squalus*, using an oscillator. This device sent a high-pitched tone under water and could be used to transmit Morse code* signals.

The piercing ping of the oscillator offered further hope to the survivors on board *Squalus*. Naquin dispatched two men to the conning tower to reply. They hammered out a response with a small sledge hammer, passing on the grim news that only 33 of the crew remained alive.

Contact

Falcon, and her rescue chamber, arrived at 4:20 the next morning, along with Allen McCann – the chamber's chief designer. By 9:30am, she had anchored herself directly above *Squalus*. A diver was then lowered into the ocean and was able to attach a thick guide cable to her escape hatch.

Everything was in place and, for the first time, the McCann Rescue Chamber was to be used in a real rescue. Momsen picked two of his best divers to go down in the bell, which was winched over the side of *Falcon*, reaching *Squalus* 15 minutes later. Steel bolts anchored it in place over the submarine's escape hatch.

"We're here!"

As *Squalus*'s hatch swung open, a blast of foul and freezing air rushed into the chamber, and a collection of dull, drawn faces looked up at their rescuers. The divers, expecting at least a cheer or welcome, were stunned by the silence that greeted them. "Well," said one, rather lost for words, "we're here!", and began to pass down soup, coffee and sandwiches.

Rescue chamber

Once guide lines had been attached by a diver, the McCann Rescue Chamber could be winched down to a sunken submarine.

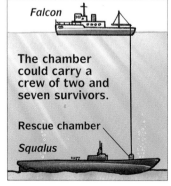

Falcon

The chamber could carry a crew of two and seven survivors.

Rescue chamber

Squalus

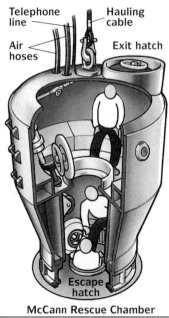

Telephone line

Hauling cable

Air hoses

Exit hatch

Escape hatch

McCann Rescue Chamber

Escape hatch. McCann Rescue Chamber docked here.

Conning tower

Control room

Forward battery room. Fumes from here nearly choked the survivors.

Forward torpedo room

Torpedo tube

192

*See page 60

Deep-sea diver

In the 1930s, divers had to wear heavy, clumsy outfits such as this and needed to be exceptionally strong.

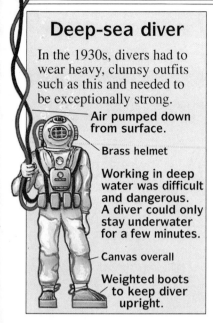

Air pumped down from surface.

Brass helmet

Working in deep water was difficult and dangerous. A diver could only stay underwater for a few minutes.

Canvas overall

Weighted boots to keep diver upright.

The McCann chamber remained attached to *Squalus* for an hour, as fresh air was pumped down from the surface. Seven men climbed inside, and after a slow ascent the chamber surfaced and was hauled aboard the *Falcon*.

Momsen and McCann were jubilant – their invention had worked. They could see no reason why the remaining 26 men on board *Squalus* should not be rescued, and the chamber was readied for a second dive.

Choking gas

But inside the submarine all was far from well. Thick, choking clouds of chlorine gas were rising from batteries contaminated with sea water. Naquin had to act quickly, before his crew were poisoned by the gas, and led them through to the forward torpedo room. The bulkhead door to the battery room was sealed. Confined to an even smaller space than before, the men resumed their cramped, huddled positions, and waited.

Reel jam

On the surface, the diving chamber had been readied for its next descent. But once in the water the cable reel jammed and the bell had to be hoisted up for a second attempt. This time nine men were rescued. A third successful trip followed, after which only eight remained in the sunken submarine.

By the time the divers were ready for a final descent, dusk had fallen and searchlights illuminated the chamber as it entered the water. Once again the docking was faultless, and the remaining eight men climbed aboard.

At 8:40pm the ascent began, but halfway up, the down-haul cable jammed. The two divers operating the chamber hit it with their fists, then kicked it with impotent rage. But they were still stuck. There was only one thing left to do – the bell would have to return to the sea bottom, where a diver could attempt to sever the jammed down-haul reel.

When this was done, the *Falcon* began to winch the chamber to the surface at a

Below. **The scene at the Isle of Shoals, May 24, 1939.** *Falcon* recovers the rescue chamber after a successful dive.

steady 1.5m (5ft) per minute. But the sea was reluctant to give up its victims. In the stark light of the searchlights, men on board the *Falcon* noticed strands in the cable begin to snap and unravel.

Momsen once again ordered the bell to descend to the sea bottom. Another diver was sent down to fasten a new cable, but he was swiftly overcome by exhaustion and had to be pulled back to the surface. Then a third diver was sent down, but he too failed to fasten a new cable.

There was now no alternative but to haul the chamber back to the surface with the frayed cable. Fearful that the steam pulley which usually hauled it in would snap it at any moment, Momsen and McCann decided the cable would have to be pulled up by hand.

Freezing haul

So, in a freezing wind and after an exhausting day, a team of sailors, hauling and relaxing the rope with the swell of the sea, began the laborious task of dragging the chamber to the ocean surface.

After 10 minutes the threadbare section of cable emerged from the sea – as thin as a piece of string. Momsen, watching with wide-eyed trepidation, found himself bathed in sweat, despite the cold.

With incredible delicacy a clamp was attached to the cable below the break, and once this was done the danger was over. Winched onto the deck at 12:30am, the final survivors of *Squalus* staggered out of the Rescue Chamber after nearly 40 hours trapped underwater. No submariners before them had been rescued from such a depth.

Hindenburg's hydrogen hell

The huge airship rose so gently into the evening sky that those on board only realized they were taking off because the waving figures on the ground appeared to be getting gradually smaller.

Standing at the windows of the observation platforms on either side of the ship, or at their stations within the huge metal and canvas framework, the 42 passengers and 55 crew on the *Hindenburg* could not fail to feel they were aboard the most extraordinary aircraft ever constructed.

Brass band departure

To mark the ship's first Atlantic crossing of 1937, from Rhein-Main World Airport, Frankfurt, a brass band in blue and yellow uniforms stood on the runway and played the German national anthem. Then, when the ship reached 90m (300ft), huge wooden propellers began to turn as four diesel engines roared into life, drowning out the band below. With a thunderous drone, the airship

vanished into the night. As the landscape of central Germany unfolded beneath them, many of the passengers spent a pleasant evening watching the gleaming beacons of small towns and villages, and huge pools of city lights, roll leisurely by.

Liner of the sky

Hindenburg was the size of an ocean liner and almost as opulent. The dining room offered such delights as Bavarian style fattened duckling and roast gosling. A lounge, complete with lightweight aluminium piano, and a bar and smoking room, provided further luxury. Passengers slept in 25 cabins lined with pearl-grey linen, each with hot

IM ZEPPELIN ÜBER DEN OZEAN

DEUTSCHE ZEPPELIN-REEDEREI

Margaret Mathen
Frankfurt
Lakehurst   13
3.5.1937

HAMBURG-AMERIKA LINIE

Passengers aboard the *Hindenburg* enjoyed a champagne lifestyle. Such luxury did not come cheap; in 1937 a round trip across the North Atlantic cost $810 – around the same price as a family car.

Left. *Hindenburg* preparing for take off, Germany, 1936.

and cold water. Like any exclusive hotel, they could even leave shoes outside their doors to be cleaned overnight.

Zeppelin veteran

In the forward control cabin sat *Hindenburg*'s captain, Max Pruss, World War One Zeppelin* veteran and seasoned airship commander. It was his responsibility to ensure the ship remained stable, a tilt of even two degrees could send wine bottles crashing from tables and play havoc with food preparation in the galley.

With Pruss in the cabin was Ernst Lehmann, director of the Zeppelin Reederei – the company which built German airships and ran the Atlantic crossings service. Business was good, and flights were now fully booked for the whole year.

Both men had every faith in their magnificent craft, but neither could fail to be aware of the fate that had overtaken almost every other huge airship during the previous few years. In 1930, Britain's *R101* had crashed in flames, and almost all on board had been killed. The USA had been no more successful at mastering these aerial giants. Two similarly huge craft had both crashed within two years of their maiden flights.

Hydrogen bomb

Despite the problems other nations faced, in six years of successful passenger flights Germany had built an enviable reputation as the only country capable of flying airships without disaster.

But even the *Hindenburg* had one potentially fatal flaw. The lighter-than-air gas that lifted it into the sky was hydrogen – the same element that burns so fiercely on the Sun. If a gas cell leaked, a mere spark could cause a blazing catastrophe.

The airship's designers had taken this into account. All meals were cooked with electricity, rather than gas. The bar, which had a smoking room, was equipped with electrical lighters and had a double door to insulate it from the rest of the ship.

Across the Atlantic

So the *Hindenburg* flew confidently on, her passage a succession of wonderful meals, washed down with the finest German wines. Flying over Newfoundland, Pruss took the airship down low, to give his passengers a good look at the beautiful icebergs that lined their way.

The flight reached New York on May 6, three days after leaving Frankfurt, and flew so close over the Empire State Building that passengers could clearly see photographers snapping away as they crossed. Strong winds delayed the trip by half a day, but otherwise the journey was uneventful.

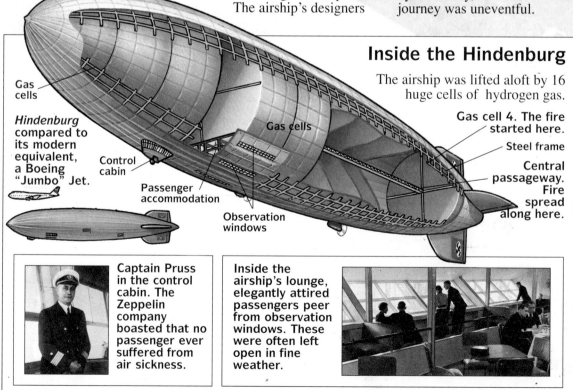

Inside the Hindenburg

The airship was lifted aloft by 16 huge cells of hydrogen gas.

Gas cells

Hindenburg compared to its modern equivalent, a Boeing "Jumbo" Jet.

Control cabin

Passenger accommodation

Gas cells

Observation windows

Gas cell 4. The fire started here.

Steel frame

Central passageway. Fire spread along here.

Captain Pruss in the control cabin. The Zeppelin company boasted that no passenger ever suffered from air sickness.

Inside the airship's lounge, elegantly attired passengers peer from observation windows. These were often left open in fine weather.

At 6:00 that evening, the *Hindenburg* approached its final destination – Lakehurst Airfield, New Jersey. Passengers gathered with their luggage in the ship's main lounge, ready to disembark. Below, over 200 ground crew readied themselves for the complex task of restraining and anchoring the huge vessel in blustery conditions.

Documenting disaster

A large crowd, including newspaper and radio journalists, had also gathered to watch her land. Among them was radio reporter Herb Morrison, broadcasting live for a Chicago radio station. His report began peacefully enough, as the airship loomed out of the evening sky and drifted down to her mooring mast...
"Here it comes, ladies and gentlemen, and what a sight it is...a thrilling one, a magnificent sight. The mighty diesel motors roar."

Blood to ice

But death was waiting for the *Hindenburg* at Lakehurst. Inside the ship, just forward of the mighty tail fins, two crewmen noticed a sight that turned their blood to ice. Lurking in the middle of the number four gas cell was a bright blue and yellow ball of curling fire.

On the ground, observers could see a faint pink glow inside the ship, which gave it a curiously transparent quality. One even likened it to a Japanese lantern. Then, within a second, the entire cell exploded with a muffled WHUMP, and fierce flames burst out of the silver canvas covering. A huge orange fireball erupted into a gigantic mushroom of smoke and flames, and began to devour the still airborne vessel. Wide-eyed with horror, Herb Morrison watched aghast, his voice turning from cool appreciation to hysteria. "It's burst into flame! Get out of the way! Get out of the way, please!... This is terrible. This is one of the worst catastrophes in the world! The flames are 500 feet into the sky."

Garish glow

Most of the passengers and crew were in the front section of the *Hindenburg*. Their first inkling of the disaster was seeing figures below scatter in panic over the wet ground, which had suddenly taken on a garish red glow. Within seconds the ship was lurching wildly and flames engulfed the passenger decks.

In the control cabin, the explosion was so muffled one officer thought a landing rope had broken. But then frenzied shouts of "Fire" alerted them to the true situation.

As hydrogen gas at the rear of the *Hindenburg* was consumed it sank rapidly, bottom down. As the stern fell, the bow rose, and passengers preparing to jump from the open observation windows saw the ground, and their chances of survival, falling rapidly away from them.

Fire from a volcano

The sharp angle of the *Hindenburg* turned its central passageway into a chimney, and a huge tongue of flame shot out of the nose "like fire from a volcano," according to one witness. Crewmen in the forward section clung hopelessly to metal girders but, scorched by the heat, lost their grip and fell into the swirling inferno. But as the fire from the rear spread throughout the structure, and gas burned off more evenly, the ship began to settle and landed on the ground with a ghastly hiss.

Herb Morrison could only take so much:
"Oh, the humanity! Those passengers. I can't talk, ladies and gentlemen...Honest, it is a

The *Hindenburg* was reduced to a burning carcass of twisted metal in 32 seconds.

mass of smoking wreckage... I am going to step inside where I can't see it. Listen folks, I am going to have to stop for a minute because I have lost my voice."

Walking miracle

Then, to the amazement of onlookers, people began to stumble and crawl from the raging conflagration. With extraordinary bravery, ground crew, who seconds before had been running for their lives, turned around and plunged into the burning wreck, "like dogs after rabbits," said one eyewitness.

Those who survived owed their lives mainly to where they were on the ship. The crewmen in the tail who had seen the fire start, dashed to safety when the stern hit the ground. Flames and heat always rise upward, so those under the explosion were in the best position to make a successful escape.

Acrobatic escape

Some passengers used their wits to save themselves. One, a professional acrobat, hung from a windowsill as the ship rose and fell, only jumping when he knew he could survive the fall. Another, finding himself lying on the ground surrounded by burning rubble, burrowed under the wet sand to safety.

Others were just lucky. One dazed, elderly woman simply walked down the ship's retractable steps, which had been broken open by the violent landing. One crew member survived the flames when a water tank burst above him, momentarily dousing a clear path away from the blaze.

One passenger, Leonhard Adelt, realized the airship was ablaze when it was 37m (120 ft) from the ground. As he contemplated jumping, the ship suddenly hit the ground with a tremendous impact which threw him and his wife against the floor. Tables and chairs piled up and blocked their exit, so they leaped 6m (20ft) from the open windows onto the soft sand below. Then their whole world went black as the airship crashed down on top of them.

Surrounded by burning oily clouds, they clawed through the white-hot metal struts and wires, feeling no pain as they struggled to find a route through. Adelt remembered, "It was like a dream. Our bodies had no weight. They floated like stars through space."

Another passenger, Margaret Mather, remembered that when the ship stood sharply on its stern she was thrown into a corner and several other people landed on top of her. Then flames, "bright red and very beautiful," blew into the passenger area. Mather

The blazing nose section of the *Hindenburg*, containing the passenger area, comes to rest.

watched others jump from the windows, but she was too stunned to move, imagining she was in "a medieval picture of hell". Then a loud cry brought her to her senses. "Aren't you coming?" shouted one of the ground crew who had dived into the flames, and out she ran.

Last to leave

In the control cabin beneath the ship, 12 officers and men were the last to leave. As white-hot metal crashed around them, they forged a path through the inferno.

Captain Pruss, attempting to rescue a trapped crewman, burned his face badly. Ernst Lehmann's injuries were more severe. He emerged from the wreckage a human torch. Onlookers beat the flames from his burning clothes as he mumbled, "I don't understand it." The future of his company had literally gone up in smoke. He died early the next morning.

The whole incident had taken a mere 32 seconds. Because the *Hindenburg* was a world famous phenomenon, and because newspaper reporters, broadcasters and newsreel staff had been present at Lakehurst in abundance, pictures and stories of the catastrophe quickly flashed around the world, and people everywhere were stunned by the tragedy.

But perhaps the most extraordinary aspect of the disaster was that 62 passengers and crew were able to walk out of the blazing wreckage and live to tell the tale.

"Breadfruit" Bligh's boatload of trouble

William Bligh, captain of the *Bounty*, began the morning of April 28, 1789 tied to a mast on the deck of his ship, surrounded by surly mutineers. The day ended with him, and 18 of his crew, adrift in a small boat in the vast, uncharted Pacific Ocean.

Fletcher Christian, his former friend, and second in command on the *Bounty*, had led a mutiny against him, shortly after a lengthy stopover in Tahiti, on the way to the West Indies. The harsh life at sea made an uncomfortable contrast with the beauty of the island and its friendly inhabitants. The mutineers wanted to return to the life they had all enjoyed ashore in Tahiti.

Bligh was partly to blame for his circumstances. He was an honest man with a strong sense of duty, but he also had a terrible temper. He subjected the ship's officers, especially Christian, to public and withering contempt, often for very minor misdeeds.

Lubberly rascals

In the days before the mutiny, his unthinking persecution of Christian intensified. He had also become unpopular with his crew, who he once addressed as "a parcel of lubberly rascals", and many of the mutineers wanted to kill him.

William Bligh, irascible captain of the *Bounty*, was a brilliant seaman and navigator.

Five days' food

Bligh was ushered off the *Bounty* with a bayonet to his chest and a musket in his back, and squeezed into the ship's launch. Here, 18 loyal members of his crew awaited him, together with five days' food and drink and a handful of navigation instruments.

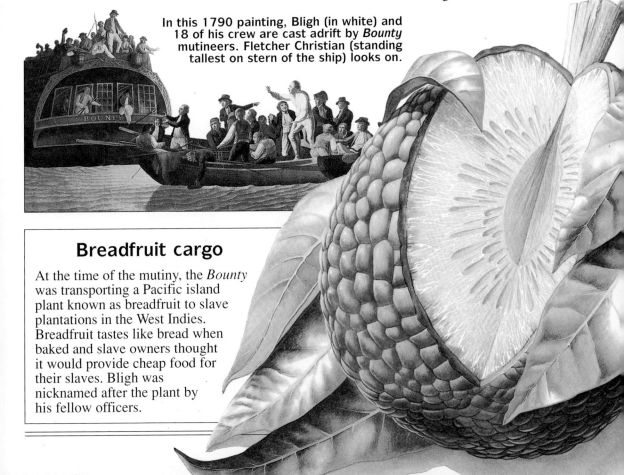

In this 1790 painting, Bligh (in white) and 18 of his crew are cast adrift by *Bounty* mutineers. Fletcher Christian (standing tallest on stern of the ship) looks on.

Breadfruit cargo

At the time of the mutiny, the *Bounty* was transporting a Pacific island plant known as breadfruit to slave plantations in the West Indies. Breadfruit tastes like bread when baked and slave owners thought it would provide cheap food for their slaves. Bligh was nicknamed after the plant by his fellow officers.

Cast adrift

The journey the castaways faced was daunting. Although their boat was equipped with oars and a sail, it was too small for the open ocean and so full that no one could lie down. The men on board were cold, wet and very hungry, they could not sleep, and had to bail water constantly to keep afloat. On top of all this, Bligh was resented by many of his fellow castaways, who felt he had brought the mutiny on himself.

But Bligh knew better than most the dangers ahead. He had sailed here with Captain Cook, the famous Pacific explorer, who had been killed by hostile islanders. He also knew the nearest safe haven was a Dutch trading colony on the island of Timor, where they could rejoin a British ship and make their way home. But this was 6,300km (3,900 miles), and maybe 50 days, away.

Tofua Island

Bligh decided their first priority would be to find food for the journey, so, despite the dangers, they landed on nearby Tofua Island, which the *Bounty* had passed by the night before the mutiny.

After a day or so, islanders arrived. They were friendly and traded food for the men's uniform buttons and beads. But when they realized they were dealing with castaways, rather than a party from an armed ship, their attitude changed.

Stone warning

Bligh's men were anxious to go, but keenly aware that their departure might provoke an all-out attack. More Tofuans had gathered at the beach and began to knock stones together in a sinister manner. Bligh had seen islanders behave like this shortly before Captain Cook was killed.

As night fell, the boat was slowly filled with supplies. Bligh's men edged toward the shore, telling the Tofuans they would sleep at sea but trade with them again in the morning. They headed for the boat, but the islanders all stood up and again began to knock stones together. As the castaways entered the water, stones rained down on them and the islanders charged.

The castaways traded beads and buttons for food.

The ship's quartermaster, John Norton, bravely turned to face their attackers and was struck down and killed, although the rest of the party managed to reach the launch. Bligh and others distracted their attackers by throwing clothes overboard. As their assailants stopped to pick these up, the boat sailed out of reach to the safety of the open sea.

Survival rations

Many other lush, green islands lined their route back to a safe European-held haven but, after such a narrow escape, any thoughts of landing on them were quickly abandoned.

Bligh realized that, to have any chance of survival, he would have to ration their provisions very carefully. Aside from the few coconuts they had brought from Tofua, the ship carried a rapidly decomposing supply of biscuits, a few pieces of salted pork, 12 bottles of rum and wine, and several barrels of fresh water.

Standing at the stern, Bligh addressed his weary boatload. Their supplies, he told them firmly, would have to last 50 days. Each man could be given only one ounce (28g) of biscuits, and a quarter pint (0.1 litre) of water a day. Then he made each of them swear before the others that he would accept the rations given to him, and not ask for more.

Hot pursuit

Something in their captain's manner must have reassured the crew, because they sailed from Tofua in good spirits. But two days later, the sun rose red and fiery – a sure sign that a storm would soon be upon them.

That morning an even more immediate threat presented itself. As they passed by the island of Waia, two sailing canoes set out after them, causing great alarm in the launch. The castaways were certain that, if caught, they would be killed and eaten.

Howling wind

Bligh ordered six men to the oars, and they rowed for their very lives. For three nerve-racking hours the canoes gave chase, only abandoning their quarry in the early afternoon. But no sooner had the crew recovered from their escape than a howling gale and torrential rain tore into the fragile boat.

The men endured a miserable, sleepless night and in the gathering light of dawn the storm showed no sign of abating. But Bligh had two remedies to comfort his crew, and they were both surprisingly effective. He instructed his numbed companions to dip their sodden clothes in the sea, which was warmer than rain, and then gave each man a spoonful of rum.

The *Bounty's* launch, from an 1824 account of the mutiny. When the wind was low, the boat could be rowed along.

Four-hour routine

Sailors cast away in open boats often succumb to a state of listless apathy. They curl up motionless, as static as their changeless circumstances. Bligh was determined to prevent this happening. He divided his men into two groups and while one group sailed the boat the other lay in the bottom and rested. These two groups switched every four hours, and this routine gave shape to what would otherwise have been a shapeless day.

Ration ritual

Bligh turned the highlight of each day – the handing out of rations at 8:00am, noon and sunset – into a lengthy ritual. The daily amount for each man was weighed out on a scale made from two coconut halves. A couple of pistol bullets served as weights and the whole process of preparing each portion kept the entire crew entranced. Biscuits were always on the menu, but Bligh kept the pork as an occasional surprise, delighting the boat by handing out tiny strips. Bligh invited his men to make their paltry ration last as long as any ordinary meal. He always broke his bread into minute morsels, and ate it very slowly.

Maps and prayers

He also entertained his men with stories about earlier voyages and encouraged them to share their own adventures. He drew maps to show where they were going and told them all he knew about the route. Every night he led the boat in pitiful prayers – "Bless our miserable morsel of bread, that it may be sufficient for our undertaking" – and tried to lift their spirits with seafarers' songs.

Bligh also instructed his crew to sew together a patchwork Union Jack flag from bundles of signal flags which had been thrown into the boat.

The daily ration of biscuits was weighed out in coconut shell scales.

Who shall have this?

Occasionally, Bligh and his crew caught a bird. This was divided among them all in a navy custom called "Who shall have this?". One man points to a morsel and another who cannot see him calls a name at random. The piece goes to that man. In this way arguments about who has which part of the bird are avoided. In his log Bligh wryly noted the "great amusement" in the boat when he was given a beak to eat.

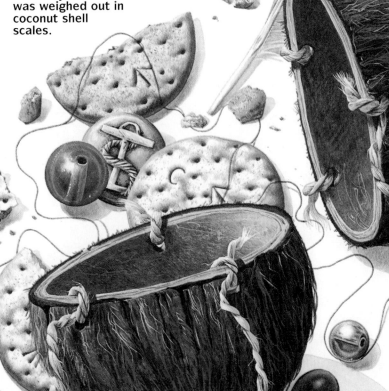

They would use the flag to identify themselves when the launch reached Kupang. It was a shrewd move. Making it kept the men occupied, but it was also a symbol of hope for the end of their ordeal.

Hunger and rain

For 15 days the tiny boat pushed on through an unbroken spell of bad weather, and the men were constantly drenched and freezing. Bligh recorded that "Our appearances were horrible. I could look no way, but I caught the eye of someone in distress. Extreme hunger was now too evident. The little sleep we got was in the midst of water, and we constantly awoke with cramps and pains in our bones".

Even worse was to come. Twenty-one days into the voyage, Bligh realized their biscuits were not going to last. The ration would have to be cut from three to two portions a day. Although the men took the news without protest, the decision, he wrote, "was like robbing them of life".

After almost a month at sea the crew began to notice signs of land. Not island land, which they had to avoid, but the huge continent of Australia (then called New Holland), where they could replenish their supplies and rest for a while, hopefully undetected.

A broken branch floated by. Many birds now wheeled around the launch. Best of all, clouds, which always form around the coast, could constantly be seen on the western horizon. When they heard the sea roaring against the rocks they knew they would soon be standing on solid ground.

Australian landfall

On May 28, the small boat passed gingerly through the Great Barrier Reef, just off the Australian coast. Although this was still unknown and hostile territory to European seamen, the men were euphoric when they landed on a deserted offshore island. Many were so weak they could hardly stand, but others tore at oysters on the rocks, guzzling down as much as they could eat.

Later that day, in a copper pot taken from the *Bounty*, a delicious stew of oysters, pork and bread was cooked, and each man had a whole pint (0.5 litre) of it to himself.

Curses and beatings

Bligh cautioned his men not to eat the fruits and berries that surrounded them. All were

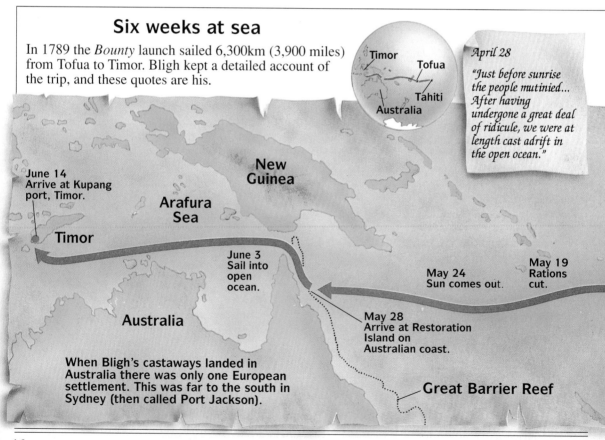

Six weeks at sea

In 1789 the *Bounty* launch sailed 6,300km (3,900 miles) from Tofua to Timor. Bligh kept a detailed account of the trip, and these quotes are his.

Timor
Tofua
Tahiti
Australia

April 28

"Just before sunrise the people mutinied... After having undergone a great deal of ridicule, we were at length cast adrift in the open ocean."

June 14
Arrive at Kupang port, Timor.

New Guinea

Arafura Sea

Timor

June 3
Sail into open ocean.

May 24
Sun comes out.

May 19
Rations cut.

May 28
Arrive at Restoration Island on Australian coast.

Australia

When Bligh's castaways landed in Australia there was only one European settlement. This was far to the south in Sydney (then called Port Jackson).

Great Barrier Reef

unknown to European botanists, and some were bound to be poisonous. But his warning was ignored. On board the boat Bligh's expert seamanship commanded a grudging respect from his resentful crew, but on land this relationship withered and bitter quarrels broke out.

Bligh felt it was his duty to return everyone safely to England. The only way to do this was to share everything between them. But other men felt that everyone should look after themselves, and be able to eat what they found, rather than contribute to a common share.

Sensing his command was slipping from him, Bligh took desperate measures. "I determined [decided] either to preserve my command or die in the attempt," he wrote in his log, and drew his cutlass on one seaman who had spoken to him rebelliously.

The do-or-die approach restored order, but it was a wretched, quarrelsome party that set sail again, on the second leg of their journey to Timor. Despite the stopover, their health soon deteriorated and by the time land was sighted, after another 10 days at sea, most men were too weak even to cheer.

When the boat arrived at Kupang port in Timor, on June 14, 1789, Bligh recorded "Our bodies were nothing but skin and bones, our limbs were full of sores, and we were clothed in rags. In this condition, the people of Timor beheld [looked on] us with a mixture of horror, surprise and pity."

Kupang arrival

From Kupang they sailed to Java and then homeward on a Dutch merchant ship. The journey to

This contemporary engraving shows the *Bounty* castaways landing at Timor.

England took nine months, and several men, weakened by their ordeal, died on the way. The quarreling continued too. Bligh had two of his crew imprisoned aboard the ship for daring to suggest he had falsified expense forms. But despite his obvious faults, and against extraordinary odds, irascible William Bligh had ensured that 11 of his crew would live to see their families again.

May 3
"We walked down the beach in a silent kind of horror (then) stones flew like a shot."

May 4
"We bore away across the sea where the navigation is but little known (and) not a star could be seen to steer by."

May 21
"We were so covered with rain and salt water, that we could scarcely see."

May 24
"For the first time, during the last fifteen days, we experienced comfort from the warmth of the sun."

June 14
"It appeared scarcely credible to ourselves that in an open boat and so poorly provided, we should have been able to reach the coast of Timor in 41 days..."

May 7
Chased by canoes from Waia Island. Storms begin.

Pacific Ocean

The launch

May 6
Pass by Fiji.

The *Bounty*

April 4
Bounty leaves Tahiti.

April 28
Mutiny occurs.

Tahiti

May 2
Launch arrives at Tofua.

Susie Rijnhart's Tibetan trek

I t had not been a successful
expedition. Journeying into
Tibet, Canadian Protestant
missionary Susie Rijnhart and
her husband Petrus had met
only disappointment and
tragedy. They had made few
Christian converts. Their
servants, fearful of the bandits
that infested the mountainous
countryside, had deserted them.
Most of their pack ponies had
been stolen. When their
11-month-old son died in the
Himalayan mountains they
almost gave up in despair, but
worse was to come.

Petrus sets off

On a frosty September morning
in 1898, in the Tanggula Shan
region, Susie Rijnhart bid
farewell to Petrus as he set off
to a nearby village on the
opposite side of the mountain
river bank where they had made
camp. Two more ponies had
been stolen and he was going
to enquire if anyone knew what
had happened to them.

As daylight turned to dusk,
Petrus did not return and
Rijnhart began to feel uneasy.
The dark, desolate stillness of
the mountains filled her with
foreboding and she could not
rid herself of the thought that
something terrible had
happened, and she was now
totally alone.

Rijnhart the missionary

Rijnhart, a Canadian doctor
of medicine, was drawn to
missionary work in the Far
East in her early thirties, and
soon mastered several
languages, including
Chinese and Tibetan.

Tibet, where the
principal religion was
Buddhism, was an
unwelcoming
place for
missionaries,
especially
women.

Rijnhart dressed in Tibetan
fashion to make herself as
inconspicuous as possible.
Europeans were almost
unknown in the region she
visited, and practically
everything she carried,
from spoons to towels,
was an item of curiosity
that could be traded
for other goods.

**Susie Rijnhart
in Tibetan
costume.**

The next day passed, and a
gnawing suspicion that her
husband was dead grew deeper.

Armed party

Another night came and went.
Next morning, as Rijnhart
stood scanning the horizon
with the telescope she always
carried, she heard shouts
behind her. Thinking it was
Petrus, her heart leaped with
joy but, instead, a party of

armed Tibetans approached.

Curt greetings were
exchanged and questions
asked. Where was her husband?
He had gone to a nearby
village she told them and
would soon return. Was she not
afraid to be alone? No, she
carried a revolver.

Rijnhart produced the gun
and explained it could fire six
shots before a bandit could fire
one. Each bullet, she told them,
could go through three men.
As a stranger in dangerous
territory she was aware of the
need to appear confident and
powerful and the horsemen
trotted off, suitably impressed.

Looking for help

Convinced now that the local
villagers had killed Petrus,
Rijnhart decided to go to the
next settlement, to try and find

Mountainous Tibet

In 1898, this icy, mountainous country
was part of the Chinese Empire. It was
a dangerous, lawless place. The few
Chinese officials who ruled the region
depended on local chiefs to keep order.
This was a very informal arrangement.
Most Tibetans led a nomadic life, taking
their tents and cattle wherever suitable.

China
—Tibet

help. Loading her belongings on her horse, she walked along the fierce-flowing river until she saw a cluster of tents on the other side. She shouted to attract attention, and waved a *khata* (bright ceremonial scarf) as a lure, but this was an inadequate bait. Only when she waved a piece of silver did someone agree to help, and she was ferried across the river on the back of a yak (a hairy mountain ox).

At first the villagers were suspicious and unfriendly, but after a couple of hours they warmed to Susie Rijnhart. She spoke their language, was respectful of their customs and kind and courteous. They were sympathetic when she told them about Petrus, but were too afraid of the nearby villagers to offer her any help.

Trip to Jyekundo

Instead, they suggested she travel to Jyekundo, where there was a Chinese official who might send soldiers to punish her husband's killers.

Jyekundo was 10 days' travel by horse, or 15 days away by yak. Rijnhart did not know the route, so she hired three villagers to act as guards and guides. Without them she would soon be lost in the bleak mountainous terrain or assaulted by ruthless robbers.

Bandit territory

The men accompanied her for five days, but the farther they got from home, the greater was their fear of attack, and eventually they turned back. But before they left they found three more local villagers for

Rijnhart's revolver was her only protection in a hostile world.

her to hire. These men were pleasant enough, but knew Rijnhart had little money. She suspected they were making deliberately slow progress, so that when she could no longer afford to pay them, they would only have a short journey home.

New plan

Stranded in such hostile territory Rijnhart knew her chances of survival would be slim, and she was determined not to be left alone. As they trudged through the mountains a large, imposing chief's hut in the valley below caught her eye, and she headed there intent on negotiating the use of new guides. She also wanted to hire horses, as these would be much quicker than the yaks they were using.

The chief was reluctant to help, but Rijnhart managed to convince him that if she died on his territory, Chinese officials would blame him for her death and punish him, so he grudgingly agreed to provide guides and horses to take her to Jyekundo.

Telescope deal

The chief was particularly taken with the telescope Rijnhart carried and was desperate to buy it. But rather than sell it, she promised to send it to him as a gift when she reached Jyekundo. This way it would be in the chief's interest to ensure she got there safely.

That evening she was introduced to her two new guides and began to wonder if the telescope was such a good guarantee for her safety after all. Both seemed sullen and, although one looked ordinary, the other, who had a shaven head, looked quite evil.

Cruel companions

They took to the road the next morning and her misgivings were thoroughly confirmed. During the day they furtively stole from her small supply of food, and that night they suggested she sleep with them. Rijnhart was revolted by their crude proposition and told them that if anything disturbed her in the night she would reach for her revolver. The men laughed cruelly and told her to be careful not to shoot their dog.

Next morning they treated her with disdain, even telling her that they were ashamed to be seen with her. But then they changed their tone.

They asked her kindly if she would like them to carry her heavy telescope. Rijnhart declined. She suspected their chief would kill them if they returned without the instrument, and that they would leave her to fend for herself as soon as they got their hands on it.

She was walking a tightrope, and could not afford to antagonize her disagreeable companions too much. Only her telescope kept them with her, and only her revolver stopped them from killing her.

Marsh retreat

As daylight faded to misty darkness, the party reached an immense marsh. All evening their horses waded through the sodden ground. Eventually they stopped on a spot of solid earth so remote that Rijnhart wondered if any human had ever been there before.

The guides were wearing their pleasant faces that night and, as they built a fire, they told her that here they were safe and she could sleep soundly with no danger from robbers. They curled up around the fire, men on one side, Rijnhart on the other, and a deadly waiting game began.

Although she was exhausted, Rijnhart knew she was in great danger. If she fell asleep in this isolated spot she would be murdered, and no one would ever know what had happened to her. Revolver in hand she prayed for the strength to stay awake.

As the fire burned to a few glowing embers, the Moon and stars shone bright in a cloudless sky, bathing the three recumbent figures in a ghostly silver light. Six times during the night the men called softly to her, and each time she answered swiftly and sharply, and received no further reply.

The party set off at dawn with the guides in an especially foul temper. Susie Rijnhart was not the pushover they imagined her to be and their patience was running out.

This photograph, taken in the 1890s, shows two typical Tibetan nomads by their tent.

They waded out of the marsh and returned to the beaten track, reaching a fork in the road by the middle of the morning. One of the guides went to nearby tents to ask for directions and returned with the distressing news that Jyekundo had been hit by a smallpox epidemic.

Both immediately refused to continue, as they were very afraid of catching the disease. Rijnhart reminded them that their lives depended on returning home with her telescope, but they replied that they would rather be killed among friends in their own village, than die among strangers in Jyekundo.

Faultless logic

Logic like this could not be argued with and put Rijnhart in quite a predicament. Someone had to take her to Jyekundo. Besides, if she dispensed with their services they would kill her on the spot. She needed time to think and suggested they stop to rest.

Searching for a compromise, one of the men suggested they take her to the town of Rashi-Gomba on a well-used trade route, and make sure she met up with a party of Chinese merchants. She could travel to Jyekundo with the merchants and they could take the telescope back to their chief.

His companion evidently disagreed with this plan. A fierce argument broke out between the two guides and swords were drawn. With exemplary Christian charity Rijnhart persuaded them to put down their weapons, promising again to hand over the telescope as soon as they met an obliging Chinese merchant.

Beauty and beasts

They pressed on, the men in a sullen sulk, Rijnhart exhausted but ever vigilant, and made

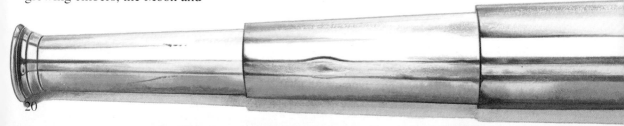

camp that night in a beautiful green valley, teeming with flocks of birds and grazing yaks. But further dangers awaited. After talking to the locals, the guides returned and told her there was a *lamasery* (Buddhist monastery) ahead where there was an intense hatred of foreigners. If she was spotted they would all be killed. Everything she had that betrayed her nationality would have to be destroyed.

More heartbreak

Rijnhart was not a conspicuous figure. She was dressed from head to toe in Tibetan clothes and her skin was burnished brown. She could hide her European features behind a large hat and scarf. Almost anything she had that was European had now been traded or stolen. But she still carried her husband's bible and diary, which she had kept with her since he disappeared, and now she faced the heartbreaking task of burying these precious mementos at the bottom of a nearby stream.

The next evening, as they

camped high in a rocky promontory, a voice called to them out of the dark. The two guides rose to meet a stranger who had been sent from the *lamasery* to investigate them. He immediately pointed to Rijnhart and asked who she was. The guides had their story ready, and it was a good one – their companion was a Chinese man who spoke no Tibetan, so there was no point talking to him. Rijnhart's hat and fur collar concealed most of her face and nothing in her appearance gave the stranger cause to doubt this story.

Safer territory

The next day was bright and sunny. As they passed through verdant countryside a light breeze rustled the leaves of the evergreen trees around them. Rijnhart felt happier for the first time since Petrus had disappeared, and the nearer she got to Rashi-Gomba, the safer she felt.

When they reached the town the guides took her to the house of a *lama* (Buddhist priest) where a Chinese merchant

stayed. Their part of the bargain completed, they snatched the telescope with a grunt and a sneer and made off, leaving Rijnhart overwhelmingly relieved to have survived their company.

Kind and helpful

This Chinese merchant was kind and helpful, and arranged for her to be presented with an official permit which guaranteed her guides and horses from any local chieftain on her way back to China.

After several weeks' travel she came to the Yangtze river, whose waters eventually flow to the Pacific Ocean. Although she was still many thousands of miles from home, she felt comforted to be by a river which reached an Ocean that shared a distant shore with her Canadian homeland.

She never was able to persuade any officials on her route to investigate Petrus' disappearance. His probable death remained a mystery.

Safe hands

Six weeks later, workers at the Roman Catholic Mission in the Chinese town of Da jian lu answered an insistent knocking at their door. Before them stood an apparently native woman – exhausted, half-starved, her clothes in rags. She seemed close to tears and all she could say was "I am Dr Rijnhart".

In safe territory, Rijnhart soon recovered from her ordeal, but she was haunted by her last glimpse of Petrus. Wading across the river which separated their camp from the village, he had turned in the sharp autumn light and shouted something she could not hear, and then vanished forever.

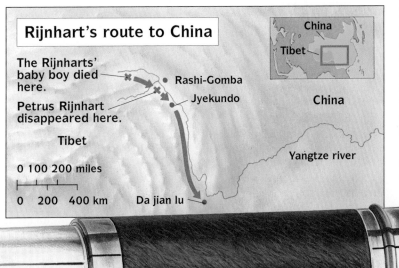

Rijnhart's route to China

China

Tibet

China

The Rijnharts' baby boy died here.

Petrus Rijnhart disappeared here.

Rashi-Gomba

Jyekundo

Tibet

Yangtze river

0 100 200 miles

0 200 400 km

Da jian lu

Mirage misery for St-Exupéry

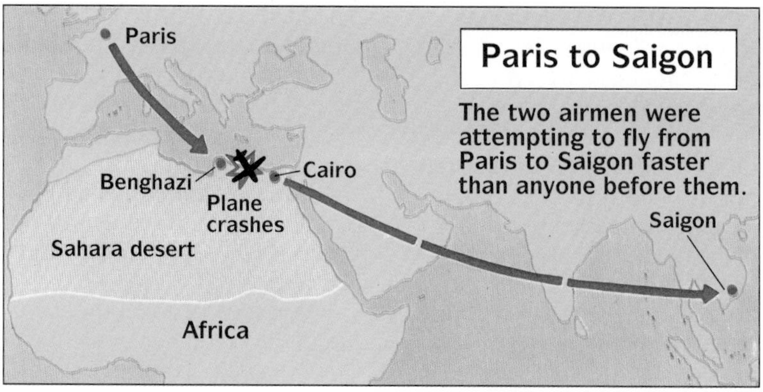

Outside the cockpit window, beyond the wing lights, the two men could see nothing but pitch black, unfathomable darkness. They were four hours out of Benghazi, en route to Cairo, and completely and hopelessly lost. Blinking away exhaustion, Antoine de Saint-Exupéry offered his copilot André Prévot another cigarette.

It was December 30, 1935. The two men were attempting to fly from Paris to Saigon* faster than anyone before them. If they broke the record before the end of the year they could claim a prize of 150,000 francs.

Saint-Exupéry, known as Saint-Ex to all, knew their lives were now in serious danger. Below lay the Sahara desert, and, with fuel rapidly running out, it was vital that they found something – a river, a city – that would give them a clue to their whereabouts.

Saint-Exupéry (left), and copilot Prévot (right), were flying between Benghazi, Libya, and Cairo, Egypt, when they crashed.

Paris to Saigon

The two airmen were attempting to fly from Paris to Saigon faster than anyone before them.

Map labels: Paris, Benghazi, Cairo, Plane crashes, Sahara desert, Africa, Saigon

Crash landing

Then, both at the same time, the two men spotted a lighthouse blinking in the darkness. They must be by the sea! Saint-Ex took the plane down low, hoping to spot a suitable place to land and ask for directions. But an instant later the plane smashed into the ground, shuddering violently as it plunged across the desert. Inside the cockpit, the flyers braced themselves for a fiery, violent death. But no explosion came, and the plane rapidly screeched to a grinding halt.

Scarcely believing they were still breathing, the two men tumbled out of the cockpit and fled for their lives.

Safely away, they ran trembling hands over their bodies, checking for broken bones. With extraordinary luck, neither had injuries worse than bruises. Looking around, it was clear why the plane had not exploded when it hit the ground. They had landed on rounded, black pebbles, rather than sand, and their aircraft had rolled along, as if it were on ball bearings.

Phantom lighthouse

So far so good, but where were they? A quick look around confirmed that the lighthouse had been an illusion – maybe an instrument light reflected in the cockpit window. The sea was nowhere to be seen.

Checking the supplies, they found the plane's water container had burst, its contents instantly soaked up by the arid ground. Between them they had a small flask of coffee, half a bottle of wine, a slice of cake, a handful of grapes and an orange.

Specks in the desert

Saint-Ex and Prévot crawled back inside the plane and waited for the dawn. Neither could sleep, their situation was too desperate. If they had crashed on a recognized flight path they might be rescued within a week. But they were completely lost – specks in a huge, sprawling desert. A search party could spend six months looking for them without success. In the heat of the day their supplies might last five hours, and Saint-Ex had been told that in such an environment a man could live less than à day without water. Both began to wonder if it would have been better to have died when their plane hit the ground.

Black pebble world

The dawn brought no relief. All around, rising and falling in dunes and hillocks, black pebbles stretched to the horizon. Not a single blade of grass grew from the ground. Their surroundings were as lifeless as the Moon.

Saint-Ex took a map from the plane and studied it forlornly. Even if they had known where they were, it would have offered little comfort. The vast emptiness of the desert was punctuated by the occasional symbol for a well, or religious institution. But these were few, and far apart.

Desert reconnaissance

It was too early to give up hope. Perhaps an oasis lay nearby? They wrote their plan for the day in huge 10m (30ft) letters in the ground, in case anyone should find the plane when they were gone, then they headed east, scraping their boots behind them to leave a trail back to the plane.

They soon forgot to mark their route, and after five hours of wandering, began to worry they would not find a way back. As the sun rose, the fierce heat drained the strength from their bones and mirages began to torment them. A faint shape on the horizon could be a fort or town? The dark shadow to the west could be vegetation? Lakes glistened in the distance, but all vanished as they approached.

Tormented by thirst

After six hours, the need to drink became the only thing that mattered, and when they stumbled over tracks left hours before, they made their way back to the plane, and the last of their supplies. The coffee and wine were quickly consumed and the two men then set about building a fire, dragging a piece of wing away from the wrecked aircraft, and dousing it with fuel.

As thick, black smoke rose into the cloudless sky, both men stared into the flames. Saint-Ex imagined he could see his wife's face looking up at him sadly from under the rim of her hat. Prévot too thought of his loved ones – and the grief his death would cause them.

Animal burrows

There was one ray of hope. Saint-Ex had found some animal burrows. Something had managed to survive in this sterile wilderness, so perhaps they could too. That night they set traps over a couple of burrows.

Next morning, they woke determined to beat the desert, and began the day by wiping

Desert maps are as empty as the areas they depict. Saint-Ex's map was useless, as he did not know where they had crashed.

dew off the wings of their plane with a rag. Rung out, it yielded only a spoonful of liquid – a sickening mixture of water, paint and oil.

New plan

Prévot decided to stay with the aircraft, where he could light a fire in case a search plane flew over. Saint-Ex would go into the desert and forage. Although his traps were empty, there were tracks nearby. Judging from the three-toed palm imprint in the sand, the animal was a desert fox. Saint-Ex followed the tracks until he came to the animal's feeding ground – a few measly shrubs, with small golden snails among the branches. The snails were probably poisonous, and there was no water to be had from the shrubs, so Saint-Ex pressed on.

Hallucinations

Thirst was taking its toll, and he was having terrible trouble deciding whether the images he could see were mirages, hallucinations, or for real. First there was a man standing on a nearby ridge. That turned out to be a rock. Then he saw a sleeping Bedouin* and rushed to wake him. This turned out to be a tree trunk. It was so weathered and desiccated it had turned to smooth black charcoal.

*Desert tribesman

Then he saw a desert convoy of Bedouins and camels moving along the horizon, and called out to the empty desert. A monastery, a city, the sound of the sea, all followed in succession. Saint-Ex was a philosophical character and, rather than be tormented by these illusions, he allowed himself to be amused. In his dazed state he staggered around happily, laughing at his circumstances.

Despair at dusk

Darkness fell, and the mirages faded. Despair swept over him. Saint-Ex cried out desperately, his hoarse voice no more than a feeble whimper, and returned empty handed to Prévot, who had lit a fire to guide him back. But in the flickering light, Saint-Ex saw something which made his heart leap. Prévot was talking to two Bedouins – they were safe! Contact had been made with people who could guide them out of the wasteland! But the two strangers vanished as he approached. Saint-Ex had seen another cruel hallucination.

Water from the air

That night, the two men tore a parachute into six sections and laid it on the ground, covered with stones to stop the wind from blowing it away. This would catch the morning dew and provide them with much-needed water. They shared an orange and slept an exhausted sleep.

Soon after dawn next morning they wrung out nearly 2 litres (4 pints) of water from the parachute fabric into the only receptacle they had – an empty petrol tank.

Unfortunately the water was horribly contaminated by both the lining of the tank, and chemicals used to treat the parachute. It was yellow-green and tasted quite revolting. Both men spent the next 15 minutes retching into the sand.

Walk into the unknown

Prévot and Saint-Ex realized that no search party was going to find them. To stay with the plane was to wait submissively for death. There was no other choice but to walk into the unknown and hope they would find something or someone who would save them.

Heading east, for no particular reason, they trudged stoically through the sand, baked by the scorching sun, heads held down, to avoid the tormenting mirages. Saint-Ex felt as if he were pursued by a wild beast, and fancied he could feel its breath in his face.

Too thirsty to swallow

By dusk they were so thirsty neither could swallow, and a thick crust of sand covered their lips. But as the sun set, Prévot saw a lake glistening on the horizon. Saint-Ex knew it was not real, but his friend was sure this hallucination was genuine, and staggered off to investigate.

Lying on his back, Saint-Ex began to daydream about the sea. Time passed and still Prévot had not returned. He stared at the Moon, which now loomed unnaturally large above him, then he saw lights in the darkness – a search party! – and shouted after them. A figure loomed out of the dark. It was Prévot. The lights were another illusion. The two men began to bicker at each other's stupidity, their frustrations boiling over into unreasonable impatience. Then they stopped. "I guess we're both in a bad way," said Prévot.

Desperate drink

Desperate for a drink, Saint-Ex's thoughts wandered to the small bottles of alcohol, ether and iodine* they carried in their medicine box. He tried the ether, but it stung his mouth sharply. The alcohol made his throat tighten alarmingly. One whiff of the brown iodine stifled any further experimentation.

Cold night

Although deserts are very hot during the day, at night they become intensely cold, and fierce winds swept over the two men. For the last three nights the plane had protected them, but now they were out in the open. Nothing in the desert offered any shelter and, having been roasted by the sun, they were now in danger of freezing

Saint-Ex and Prévot were so desperate to drink, they tried the poisonous liquids in their medicine box.

*These are used as ointments and are very poisonous.

to death. In desperation, Saint-Ex dug himself a shallow trough and covered his body with sand and pebbles, until only his head stuck out. As long as he stayed still, the cold did not cut into him.

Grave reminder

For Prévot, a hole in the ground was all too reminiscent of a grave, and he tried to keep warm by walking around and stamping his feet. He also built a feeble fire with a few twigs, but this soon went out.

The night seemed to go on forever, and when dawn finally came there was no dew. But at least they could still speak. When people are dying from thirst and exhaustion their throats close up and a bright light fills their eyes. Neither man was in that state, so they hurried off, determined to travel as far as possible before the sun got too hot.

Ceased to sweat

By now, both men were so dehydrated, they had ceased to sweat. As the sun rose in the sky, Saint-Ex became weaker and started to see flashes of light before his eyes. A French folksong, *Aux marches du palais* ("To the steps of the palace"), played constantly in his head, but he could not remember the words.

As they struggled on, their legs began to buckle beneath them and the horrible taste in their mouths was a constant torture. The urge to lie down in the soft sand and sink into an endless sleep became overwhelming.

But then a sixth sense told them life was nearby. A ripple of hope passed between the men "like a faint breeze on

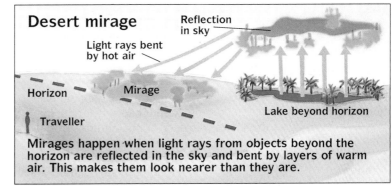

Desert mirage

Reflection in sky

Light rays bent by hot air

Horizon

Mirage

Traveller

Lake beyond horizon

Mirages happen when light rays from objects beyond the horizon are reflected in the sky and bent by layers of warm air. This makes them look nearer than they are.

the surface of a lake," as Saint-Ex later recalled. Ahead were footprints! They could hear noises! Saint-Ex saw three dogs chasing each other, and pointed joyously to them. But Prévot did not see them. They were another illusion.

Then they both saw a Bedouin on a camel. They began shouting and waving, but their voices were too feeble to be heard and the apparition disappeared behind a sand dune. But then another Bedouin appeared, and this time he saw them. To the delirious men he looked like a god walking toward them.

Great good luck

The Bedouin who found them knew exactly what to do with survivors who have been marooned in a desert without water for three days. Placing his hands on their shoulders he made them lie in the sand. He unstuck their parched lips with a feather

and gently rubbed mashed lentils into their gums, to moisten their mouths.

Only then did the Bedouin bring them a basin of water, but he had to keep pulling their heads back to stop them from drinking too quickly.

Prévot and Saint-Ex were lucky to be found by these desert wanderers and not to have stumbled on some source of water on their own. They would have drank frenziedly, and the insides of their parched mouths would have split open.

The two exhausted airmen were placed on a camel and taken to a nearby settlement. Against all expectations they had survived for three days in the fierce heat of the desert.

After his rescue, Saint-Exupéry revisits the scene of the crash.

Beware the savage beast

Killer's rubber feast

The great white shark is one of the most feared creatures in the world. So perfect is this ocean killer that it has ruled its domain since the days of the dinosaur.

The great white usually hunts fish and dolphins in the open ocean, but occasionally it will follow prey into shallow waters.

On a cool summer morning in 1991, surfer Eric Larsen, 32, sat astride his surfboard. Alone in the coastal waters of northern California, he noticed a huge, ominous shape drift effortlessly by. Within an instant his left leg had been seized by a great white shark.

Massive jaws

Larsen, who was wearing a wetsuit and gloves, instinctively thrust his hands down to wrench open the massive jaws. He was an exceptional athlete, and his great physical strength was now invaluable. The jaws inched apart, and Larsen freed his leg, only to have both arms snapped into the jagged mouth.

Pulling for his life he managed to wrench his shredded right arm free, and smashed his fist into the shark's belly. The startled animal released its grip and launched itself at Larsen's board. For a few frantic seconds, the unfortunate surfer, tethered to his board by a short cord, was heaved through the water. Then, the shark was gone.

Larsen's injuries were severe. His left leg and both arms were torn to the bone, and he was bleeding badly from the main artery in his left arm. But he was a skilled paramedic and knew exactly what he must do.

Fighting to stay calm, Larsen struggled to mount his board and headed for the shore. The temptation to paddle as fast as possible was overwhelming but Larsen knew this would make his heart beat faster and he would bleed more. Moreover, the extra blood in the water might coax the shark into another frenzied attack. His measured pace paid off. He reached the safety of the beach, and began to drag himself to houses nearby.

During an attack, the great white changes the shape of its mouth.

Snout lifts up.

Upper jaw protrudes from mouth.

Sharks have the biggest teeth of all fish. No other animal has a more formidable bite.

Out of the water, Larsen clamped his right hand firmly over the spurting gash of his bleeding artery and held his left hand above his head. Wounds bleed less when blood has to flow against gravity.

As he dragged himself toward the nearest house the world spun around him, and he collapsed. But two local residents had heard his cries, and ran to help.

Larsen explained exactly what they needed to do. His shredded leg needed to be raised above his body, to slow the flow of blood, and he showed one of his helpers where to press down on his arm to restrict the blood still pouring out of him.

Local emergency services arrived soon after, and an hour later he was in hospital. A blood transfusion, five hours of surgery, and 200 stitches saved his life.

Despite his brush with death, Larsen soon returned to surfing. He credited his escape from one of nature's most ferocious predators to the unpleasant taste of his rubber wetsuit.

Honeybee horror for truck driver Shane

Most animal attacks on people are ferociously swift, but the ordeal that truck driver John Shane faced was agonizingly slow. In May 1992, Shane, 46, was delivering 250 beehives to a beekeeper in Florida. Shortly after midnight a collision with an oncoming car overturned his truck, leaving his bruised body covered in shattered glass and trapped in twisted metal.

There were five million bees aboard the mangled truck and they soon started to swarm. In the dark interior of his cab, the trapped truck driver began to feel hot, pin-like jabs on his neck and face, as the angry insects instinctively attacked the nearest living creature. Shane was used to working with bees. He knew that stinging bees released a scent which encouraged other bees to sting. He also knew that few people were strong enough to survive more than 200 successive stings.

Police and fire crews quickly arrived, but their flashing lights and sirens seemed to make the swarm even angrier. Two firemen began to try to free Shane from his cab. They too were persistently stung, and progress was terribly slow.

Useful advice

After a while, a local beekeeper arrived and was able to offer the rescuers useful advice. All lights were turned off and the truck was sprayed with a constant jet of water, which seemed to calm the frantic bees. But Shane knew the swarm would grow angrier as dawn broke, and he still seemed to be hours away from being freed.

His desperation grew as a bee crawled in and out of his ear, and his patience finally snapped. He called to the cutting crew and persuaded them to hand over their equipment. He would attempt to cut himself free. It was worth a try and, after a long struggle, Shane was able to cut away the steering wheel which pinned him to his seat.

As a faint glimmer of light played on the eastern horizon, he was pulled from his cab and rushed to hospital. He had been trapped and stung for a horrific 196 minutes, but apart from multiple bee stings, his injuries were confined to sprains, cuts and bruises.

Ali's treetop tiger tussle

When Subedar Ali, 29, an elephant handler at the Corbett National Park, India, was attacked by a tiger in February 1984, he felt his last moments had come. Ali, foraging for animal fodder with his colleague Qutub and two elephants, was up a tree a short distance away from his workmate when the tiger pounced and pulled him to the ground.

The animal grabbed the back of Ali's neck, then bit off the top of his scalp. As it chewed at the morsel, Ali tried to scramble away, but a swat from the tiger's huge paw pinned his leg quite firmly to the ground.

Ali knew that nothing he could do would make matters worse. Inches away from the huge animal, and enveloped in an all pervasive catty stench, he grabbed its tongue. The cat looked perplexed and then promptly bit his hand. Howling in agony, the elephant handler began to beat at the tiger's head with his other hand.

Dragged into forest

Rather than killing him instantly the tiger merely swept a magisterial paw across Ali's face, and then sank its teeth into his back, dragging him into the forest. It dropped him and paused. It seemed puzzled by its rebellious prey.

Ali seized this moment to call for help, but his companion Qutub dismissed his desperate cry as a practical joke. Fortunately, at that moment, his elephant caught the tiger's scent and reeled in terror. Qutub, atop his mount, lumbered toward Ali, shouting angrily at the savage predator. Alarmed, it backed away, allowing Ali time to call for his own elephant, who bent down low to let him crawl to safety on its back.

Ali's encounter with the tiger cost him six months in a local hospital, but its encounter with Ali cost the tiger its freedom. After the attack it was captured and spent the rest of its life in an Indian zoo.

Space catastrophe for unlucky 13

On the evening of April 13, 1970, on a flight that began at 13 minutes past the 13th hour of the day, an oxygen tank inside the American spacecraft *Apollo 13* exploded violently. In the ship's tiny command module the crew heard a loud bang and felt the ship shudder. A shrill alarm filled the capsule and control panel warning lights began to flash, indicating vital power and oxygen supplies were fast ebbing away.

The astronauts, on their way to make America's third Moon landing, had been trained to keep a cool head, but their first radio message to NASA* headquarters in Houston, USA, sounded distinctly edgy. "OK, Houston, we've had a problem."
They were 330,000km (205,000 miles) from Earth.

Pre-flight, Swigert, Lovell and Haise (from left) meet the press.

into the vacuum of space.

The crew, and staff at Mission Control, Houston (where every aspect of the flight was being carefully monitored), were bewildered. Engineers had assumed that anything which knocked out two oxygen tanks would also annihilate the spaceship. One senior engineer summed up their strategy for such an event: "You can kiss those guys goodbye". But the crew were still very much alive.

Apollo crew

Apollo 13 carried three men. Commander Jim Lovell, 42, on his second trip to the Moon, was America's most experienced astronaut. His good fortune was legendary – "If Jim fell in a creek," said a colleague, "he'd come up with a trout in his pocket." In the depths of this disaster, fate was still smiling on him. Although his fellow crewmen were new to space, they both had other experience which would now be invaluable. Command module pilot Jack Swigert, 38, was an expert on *Apollo* emergency procedures. Lunar module pilot Fred Haise, 36, had spent 14 months in the factory that built his spacecraft. He knew it inside out.

Switch trouble

The oxygen tank – a vital part of the spaceship's fuel system – had exploded when a heating switch malfunctioned. The trouble this caused abruptly doubled, when another oxygen tank linked to it emptied out

Space breakdown

At first the crew did not realize just how seriously *Apollo 13* had been damaged. But 14 minutes after the explosion, Lovell noticed a cloud of white gas drifting past a window. This was oxygen – an essential part of *Apollo 13*'s fuel supply. So much had been lost that it now enveloped the ship like a cloak. An icy fear settled in the pit of his stomach as he realized *Apollo 13* could become his tomb, locked in a perpetual orbit between Earth and Moon.

Instruments indicating power and oxygen supplies were now all heading determinedly to zero. The command module was close to breaking down and would only keep the crew alive for a couple of hours. To survive they needed to move into the craft which was to have landed them on the Moon – the lunar module. This part of *Apollo 13* had so far remained unused. Now hundreds of switches had to be operated to bring the

Mission Control at Houston, during the *Apollo 13* mission. (Astronaut Fred Haise can be seen on the TV screen.) From here hundreds of technicians monitored every aspect of the flight, and were in constant radio contact with the crew.

*NASA – America's space agency the National Aeronautics and Space Administration.

Apollo 13 – 3,000 tons of technology

The *Apollo* spacecraft could take three astronauts to the Moon. It was an unwieldy looking machine made up of three connecting sections, and was blasted into space on top of a huge *Saturn 5* rocket.

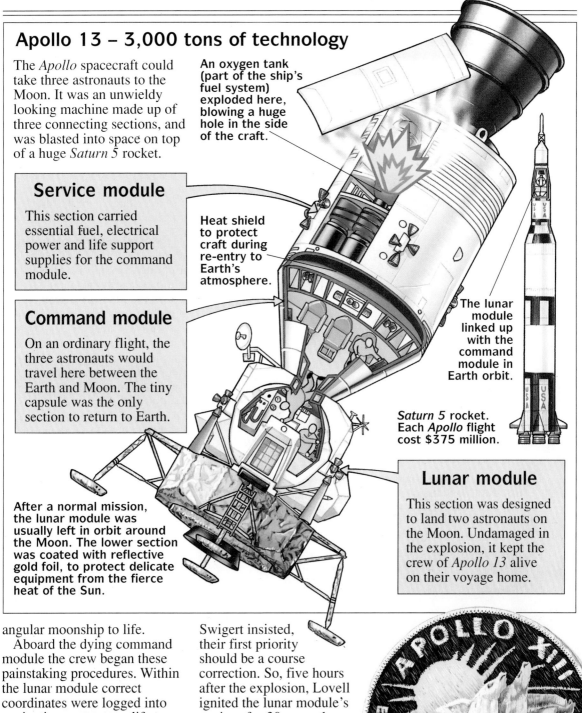

An oxygen tank (part of the ship's fuel system) exploded here, blowing a huge hole in the side of the craft.

Service module

This section carried essential fuel, electrical power and life support supplies for the command module.

Heat shield to protect craft during re-entry to Earth's atmosphere.

Command module

On an ordinary flight, the three astronauts would travel here between the Earth and Moon. The tiny capsule was the only section to return to Earth.

The lunar module linked up with the command module in Earth orbit.

Saturn 5 rocket. Each *Apollo* flight cost $375 million.

Lunar module

This section was designed to land two astronauts on the Moon. Undamaged in the explosion, it kept the crew of *Apollo 13* alive on their voyage home.

After a normal mission, the lunar module was usually left in orbit around the Moon. The lower section was coated with reflective gold foil, to protect delicate equipment from the fierce heat of the Sun.

angular moonship to life.

Aboard the dying command module the crew began these painstaking procedures. Within the lunar module correct coordinates were logged into navigation computers, life-support systems whirred into operation and instrument panels flickered into life. The men worked as hastily as they dared. A mistake made here could prove fatal.

Shifting to the lunar module solved the immediate problem of keeping them alive. Now,

Swigert insisted, their first priority should be a course correction. So, five hours after the explosion, Lovell ignited the lunar module's engines for 30 seconds, putting them on a flight that would take them around the Moon and back to Earth as quickly as possible.

All Apollo flights had their own emblem. The Latin motto *Ex Luna Scientia* means "knowledge from the Moon"

Lunar lifeboat

The crew then set about assessing their situation. The lunar module had been designed to keep two men alive on the Moon for two days. Now it would have to sustain three men for the four-day return journey. The supply situation looked like this...

• Power (electricity and fuel). Bad. This was where the explosion had done the most serious damage.

   • Food. Bad. Most was freeze-dried. It required hot water, which was no longer available, to make it edible.

   • Air. Good. There was enough to last until *Apollo 13* returned to Earth.

   • Water. Bad. All of the craft's electronic systems generated heat. Without water to cool them, they would overheat and fail.

Bare essentials

The simple truth was that the most durable items on *Apollo 13* were the three astronauts. They would be able to keep going on little or no heat or fuel for longer than any of the ship's equipment. In practical terms, this meant severe hardship for the crew. There was barely enough power to supply their essential equipment, so heating the craft became an expendable and unaffordable luxury.

As the cabin temperature dropped to half its normal level, the astronauts began to suffer. They were ill-equipped for such conditions. Their clothing and sleeping bags were intended for a warm environment, and made of thin, light materials. Improvising as best they could, the men wore two sets of underwear under their jumpsuits and Moon boots on their freezing feet.

The gnawing cold chilled the moisture in their breath and a clammy dampness settled on the spacecraft's interior. They began to feel, said Lovell, "as cold as frogs in a frozen pool."

No comfort for crew

Balanced on a knife edge between survival and an icy, suffocating death, there was little to comfort the crew. Hot food was unavailable, and the cold and worry prevented any of them from sleeping for more than two or three hours at a time. The shortage of drinking water was less of a trial, as space voyagers do not feel thirsty, although their bodies still need water. To conserve as much as possible, the men drank virtually no water at all for the rest of the flight and became dangerously dehydrated.

On the night of April 14, as *Apollo 13* swung around the Moon, the crew prepared to make a second course correction. As Lovell ran through the complex procedures needed to ignite the engines, he was astonished to notice Swigert and Haise busy photographing the Moon's surface. "If we don't make this next move correctly," snapped Lovell, "you won't get your pictures developed." Swigert and Haise were unrepentant. "You've been here before," they said, "and we haven't."

Lethal atmosphere

But once around the Moon, another deadly problem confronted them. As well as supplying its crew with air to breathe, a spacecraft also needs to remove the poisonous carbon dioxide which they exhale with every breath. In an enclosed area this can soon build up to fatal levels. Carbon dioxide filters aboard the lunar module could not cope with the amount the three men were producing.

Back on Earth, NASA technicians had been working on a solution and came up with an ingenious idea. There were several carbon dioxide filters in the now empty command module. These could be removed, placed in an airtight box, and used to filter the air aboard the lunar module.

Poisoning averted

As there were no airtight boxes aboard *Apollo 13*, the astronauts would have to improvise with storage bags, tape, air hoses and the covers of *Apollo 13*'s flight manuals. Instructions were radioed up to the beleaguered spacecraft, the contraption was built and the danger of carbon dioxide poisoning was averted.

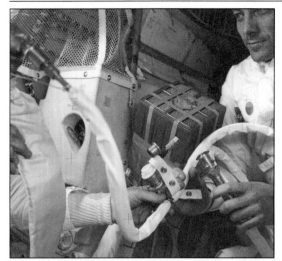

Jack Swigert assembles the makeshift carbon dioxide filter.

Final hurdle

After four days, *Apollo 13* was well on the way home, "whistling in like a high-speed train," said Swigert. One final, formidable hurdle remained – re-entry into Earth's atmosphere.

Even today, re-entry remains one of the most dangerous parts of a space mission. If *Apollo 13* approached on too steep a flight path, then it would burn up like a meteor as it hit the Earth's atmosphere. If the flight path was too shallow, it would bounce off into space, like a spinning pebble skimming across a lake. The margin for error was just a degree and a half wide.

This was not the crew's only problem. *Apollo 13* was to land in the Pacific Ocean (all American spaceships landed at sea in the 1970s) and rescue vessels had to be close at hand. To land in the right place, they would have to find a single spot above the Earth's atmosphere, called the "entry corridor", that was only 16km (10 miles) wide. Re-entry would be particularly difficult for *Apollo 13*. As with all *Apollo* spacecraft, the only section that was designed to come back to Earth was the command module, so the crew had to leave the relative safety of the lunar module and return to the crippled craft, left unused for the last four days. The command module was now as cold as a refrigerator. Water droplets had formed on every surface, from seat harnesses to instrument panels. Lovell wondered if the electronics behind the panels were just as waterlogged. They were so low on power that their equipment, if it worked at all, would have to work first time.

New instructions

Usually the command module engines would place the ship in the right position for re-entry. This time the lunar module engine would have to do it – a task it had never been designed for. At Mission Control, technicians prepared a new set of re-entry calculations and position shifts, and these were radioed up to the crew. NASA would usually take three months to prepare such a schedule, this one they put together in two days.

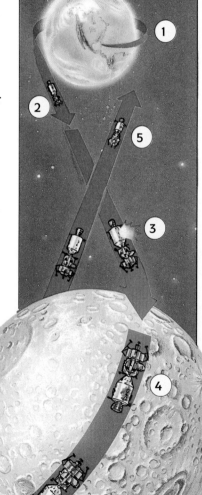

Flight to disaster

1. Lift off from Cape Kennedy, Florida, USA. April 11, 1970.

2. Leave Earth orbit. April 11.

3. Oxygen tank explodes 330,000km (205,000 miles) from Earth. April 13.

4. Mission abandoned. Lunar module engines steer *Apollo 13* around Moon, and set course to Earth. April 14.

5. Crew leave lunar module and prepare for re-entry. April 17.

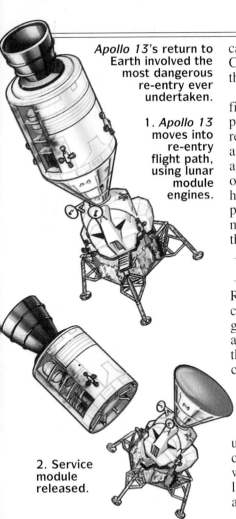

Apollo 13's return to Earth involved the most dangerous re-entry ever undertaken.

1. *Apollo 13* moves into re-entry flight path, using lunar module engines.

2. Service module released.

cavity. Lovell told Mission Control that one whole side of the craft was missing.

Now, having placed them firmly in the correct re-entry position, only the lunar module remained to be cast off. As the astronauts watched it drift away, they felt a strong surge of affection for the craft which had saved their lives. Then they prepared themselves for the most dangerous 20 minutes of their lives.

Broken communication

Re-entry is always a time when communications between ground control and spacecraft are broken. The turbulence of the air around the blazing hot craft makes radio transmission impossible. At Mission Control, technicians waited anxiously by their consoles. Three minutes passed – the usual gap in re-entry communication – and nothing was heard. Then, a minute later, Swigert's voice, muttering a terse "OK," came over the

radio. The men had survived. Bizarrely, it had rained within the capsule, as the upheaval of re-entry had loosened the water droplets within the craft.

Parachute landing

One final uncertainty lay between survival and catastrophe. Hurtling toward the Pacific Ocean, the astronauts lay strapped to their seats, wondering if there was enough power left to operate the parachutes which would slow their craft to a safe landing speed.

Four minutes later a nearby rescue helicopter relayed live video pictures to Houston, confirming that the chutes had opened. *Apollo 13* astonished the world by landing only 5.5 km (3.5 miles) away from its rescue ship – the nearest to date of any *Apollo* flight.

Below. Safely back on Earth, the *Apollo 13* crew squeeze out of their floating craft onto a life raft dropped by a circling helicopter.

Re-entry

Aboard *Apollo 13* the crew struggled to understand these new instructions. In 1970 the fax machine was still too primitive to be worth installing in a spacecraft, and Swigert took two hours to write all the hundreds of procedures down in full. He was not sure that he would understand abbreviations in the tense moments to come.

As re-entry drew closer, the damaged service module was finally uncoupled. Looking out at the silver cylinder as it slowly floated away from them, the crew saw for the first time how much damage had been caused. At the site of the explosion a tangle of wires dangled from a ruptured metal

3. Lunar module released.

4. Re-entry. When the command module hit Earth's atmosphere the heatshield had to withstand temperatures of 5,000°F (2,750°C).

Heatshield

5. Parachutes open at 7,000m (23,000ft) to slow Apollo to a safe landing speed.

6. Splashdown. *Apollo 13* floats in the Pacific Ocean. Crew await rescue by ship and helicopter.

Simpson's icy tomb

Joe Simpson woke soon after dawn, in a snow hole near the summit of Siula Grande, in the Peruvian Andes. He and climbing partner Simon Yates had burrowed this shelter when night overtook them on the return journey to their base camp, 16km (10 miles) away in the valley below. The climb up the mountain had been difficult. Disaster had trailed them like a stalking predator, and a fierce storm on the summit had almost claimed their lives. Perhaps today would be easier.

Joe Simpson

Simpson broke a small hole in the thin wall of ice above his head, and bright sunlight streamed in to bathe his face. He breathed in lungfuls of crisp, chilly air, which quickly dispelled the warm, sleepy atmosphere of the burrow.

Framed in his icy window, stretching as far as the horizon, were the peaks of South America's most formidable mountains. Dark shadows shaded their folds and fissures. Snowdrifts and glaciers gleamed blue-white in the sharp light of early morning.

Search for solid ground

As they left their snow hole shelters to set off down the mountain, they could see the descent was lined with hazardous drifts and crevasses. Wearily, they searched for solid ground, both feeling they had bitten off more than they could chew.

They hammered in toe-holds down the ice cliff that led from the summit. Progress was slow. Simpson gingerly picked a route down, clinging to the wall with ice axe and crampons*. Then, without warning, the ice cracked and he lurched into space.

Shattering agony

Simpson was linked to Yates with a climbing rope, so he did not fall far, but he crashed hard into the rock face below. His right knee shattered in fiery, explosive agony, and the intense pain made him scream out loud. Nausea swept through his body.

Yates clambered down to his injured companion as quickly as he could. One look at Simpson's misshapen, swollen knee told him his friend was as good as dead. On such a dangerous mountain, the two of them faced one of a climber's worst nightmares: Simpson was too badly injured to get back to base unassisted, Yates could easily kill himself if he helped. There was no chance of rescue.

Abseil down

Despite the extreme risk, Yates could not abandon his companion, so he worked out a technique to lower him off the mountain. For 900m (3,000ft) they abseiled down the steep slope. Yates fashioned a hollow in the snow, and sitting in it, gradually let out rope as Simpson slid down. Then, when the rope was paid out, Simpson anchored himself to the slope, and dug another hollow for Yates. Sliding down like this was incredibly painful, and the agony Simpson felt in his knee was made worse by nausea and light-headedness.

Ice axe

Yates too was suffering. His hands were black with frost bite, and the strain of lowering Simpson down the mountain was wearing him out. But after nine hours the two had made progress and had almost cleared the steepest section of the mountain. Simpson began to feel he might get out of this alive. But this dawning optimism was shattered by a catastrophe even worse than his initial fall.

As Yates let out the rope on another agonizing slide down, Simpson saw a sharp drop loom before him. He tried desperately to stop, but the ground disappeared beneath him and he plunged over an overhanging cliff face.

The situation was horrific. Yates, wedged in a snow hollow above the cliff face, did not have the strength to pull his friend back out. Simpson

*Metal frames with spikes, that can be strapped to climbing boots.

dangled 4.5m (15ft) down, 3m (10ft) away from sheer ice walls. The drop below receded 30m (100ft) into icy shadow, and the gaping mouth of a large crevasse.

As Simpson dangled, the cold ate into his bones, and he became sluggish and light-headed. The struggle to get off the mountain had failed, and he waited for death to take him.

Yates too was slowly dying of cold. Soon he would be too weak to maintain his grip and, unless he cut the rope, both of them would die. Hope faded with the falling dusk. With grim determination Yates took out his knife and sliced through the rope. Dangling in space for over an hour, Simpson had been lost in an almost pleasant semi-consciousness. Above him he could see stars in the night sky twinkling like precious stones. But then the stars went out and he plunged into the dark chasm below.

Simpson waited for the impact of his landing to crush the life out of him. But instead he just felt an intense pain in his leg, and realized that he must still be alive. He had not plummeted to the bottom of the crevasse, but had fallen 18m (60ft) down it onto a ledge.

Ice prison

Shining a flashlight around his new surroundings, Simpson could see a huge cavern of snow and ice – as still and silent as a deserted cathedral. The walls of his prison were 15m (50ft) apart, blue, silver and green, and stretched 18m (60ft) above his head to a tiny hole to the outside world, where he had fallen through. Below the ledge the steep walls were swallowed by a forbidding darkness.

Joe Simpson was expecting to die, but he had hoped to have his life dashed out of him in a brief, violent flurry. He never expected to be stranded in a crevasse, with a mangled leg, left to gradually fade away in a delirious twilight of thirst, hunger and pain.

Severed strands

He tugged the rope, and it fell down on him. Simpson could tell from the cleanly severed strands that Yates had cut the rope, but he knew that his friend had had no choice.

The night dragged on and Simpson cried to himself. When morning finally arrived with a bright beam of sunlight fanning into the roof of his icy cage, he shouted desperately for help.

But Simon Yates had gone. After he cut the rope, he burrowed into the snow to sleep, and then set off for base camp at dawn. He knew that cutting the rope was the only thing he could have done, and he had assumed that the fall down the crevasse had killed his wounded companion.

Simpson realized he was stuck there alone. He could not climb up, and he did not want to fade away slowly on the ledge. The only option left was to go down. The severed rope was at least 46m (150ft) long. He anchored it to the ledge with an ice piton (screw) and lowered himself into the gloom. He did not even look down to see what was below. If he came to the end of the rope without reaching ground, he would just let himself fall into oblivion.

Snow floor

But luck was with him. When Simpson did look down he saw a snow-covered floor. It ran the whole length of the crevasse and sloped up away from him to a sunlit crack at the top. Here was a route out!

Then he noticed black holes in the snow, and realized that this was not a floor he was hanging above – it was a drift of snow across the divide!

He had no other choice but to lower himself gingerly into the snow. He tried to put as little pressure as possible on his mangled leg, and gently, gently, he dropped onto the crisp white carpet. As the rope went slack, he found that the drift would take his weight,

Simpson attached his severed rope to an ice piton.

and he sat totally still for five minutes, hardly daring to move. Then, spread-eagled on his stomach, he began to wriggle slowly toward the distant sunlight.

Muffled thumps below jarred every nerve in his body. This noise was snow beneath him, dislodged by his movements, falling into the depths of the crevasse.

He pressed on, hoping the snow would not crumble. The slope stretched 45° up to the ceiling for maybe 40m (130ft). The final 6m (20ft) looked even steeper – maybe 65°. If he had been fit, the climb would have taken 10 minutes, but with his damaged leg it took five hours. Digging his ice axe into the snow, and inching up the slope, his sobs and curses echoed around this strange, unearthly world.

Outside world

Finally he reached the top, unhooked the rope and emerged to slump exhausted into the outside world. The bright blue sky, hot sun, and awesome ridges and folds of the surrounding mountains overwhelmed his senses, and he lay dazed in a shattered stupor.

Simpson had beaten the crevasse, but was he any better off than he had been inside it? He had no food or water, he was dying of exhaustion, his leg was useless and now frostbite had begun to disable his fingers.

Enter the voice

But Simpson was not going to give up now. An extraordinary change came over him. He began

to hear a voice in his head telling him clearly what he must do.

The voice told him to go to the glacier below. Dragging his shattered limb behind him, he crawled off, tumbling down snowy slopes, and crying out in agony every time he snagged

Simpson breaks leg here. — Siula Grande

Crevasse

Base camp

Crevasse dungeon

Simpson's fall into the crevasse, and his escape route.

1. Simpson falls through snow roof of crevasse.

2. Fall broken by ice ledge.

3. Using severed rope, Simpson lowers himself down to snow floor.

4. Route to surface.

5. Exit hole.

Crevasse beneath snow floor.

Snow floor

his leg. All day he continued, convinced that as long as he obeyed the voice he would be alright.

He passed an uncomfortable night in a snow hole, and pressed on. By early afternoon on the next day the snow thinned out, and he had reached the lower rocky slopes of Siula Grande.

Here he would have to hobble instead of crawl. Using his sleeping mat, he made a crude bandage and strapped it to his injured leg. After a couple of attempts he managed to hobble forward, using his axe as a walking stick.

The trip through the rocks was even more agonizing than the crawl through the snow. The day dragged on, but eventually the shadows grew long and cold, and it was night once again.

Too weary to stand

Next morning the voice forced him to his feet. It told him that if he did not return to camp that day he would die. Although he was totally exhausted he struggled on, muttering deliriously, his strength completely gone.

Day slowly turned to night and rain began to fall. Then, he saw flashing lights. Conversation drifted up to him, from far away. Was this a hallucination? He called out desperately, and they shouted back. A bobbing light flashed before him, as Simon Yates ran up to him with a flashlight.

Simpson could not speak. Retching, sobbing, giggling, tears streaming down his face, he had dragged himself from the very jaws of death, and now he was safe.

Death or glory for "Last Gladiator"

With his blue alligator hide shoes, white leather suit, and gold-topped cane, motorcycle stunt rider Robert "Evel" Knievel (pronounced Kuh-nee-val) was the stuff legends are made of. Over 300 jumps across snake pits, lion cages, fountains and trucks, before hordes of paying customers, had brought Evel a Rolls Royce and an income of $500,000 a year.

Of course, there were some disadvantages to the job. In five years of stunt riding, 11 serious crashes had left him with one leg slightly shorter than the other and over one hundred broken bones, held together with steel joints and screws. Evel was philosophical. Quizzed by a perplexed reporter he swaggered "I'm a competitor. I face the greatest competition any man can face, and that, my friend, is death."

Final challenge

But Knievel was becoming weary of his death or glory life on the road. Wife Linda and three children were tempting him to hang up his crash helmet before he made one jump too many.

Still, there was one final challenge the great competitor had yet to face. For years he

Stunt rider "Evel" Knievel meets the press prior to his Snake River jump, September, 1974. The former safecracker and jailbird told reporters "If it doesn't work, I'll spit the canyon wall in the eye just before I hit."

had wanted to hurtle up a ramp at full throttle, launch himself into the blue sky and power his bike from one side of a canyon to another. A scheme like that would sell enough tickets to pay for a very comfortable retirement.

Navaho veto

The Arizona Grand Canyon was the ideal choice. A national landmark, and the greatest chasm on the face of the Earth.

But the Navaho Indians, who owned the land, considered it sacred and would have nothing to do with a gaudy showbiz prankster like Knievel. Even $40,000 wouldn't make them change their minds.

The Snake River canyon in Idaho would do instead. It was 1.6km (1 mile) across and its dark jagged walls, and even darker river, made a suitably sinister spot for Knievel's last stand. Land was leased, and former NASA rocket engineer John Truax was commissioned to design a vehicle to cross it.

Million dollar rocket

Truax presented Knievel with the *Sky Cycle*. It may have been called a cycle, after Knievel's usual mode of stunt transportation, but it was in fact one million dollars' worth of steam-powered rocket. The plan was simple, Knievel would sit in this projectile, and be fired up a ramp and over the gaping mouth of the canyon. Once across, a parachute would slow the *Sky Cycle*'s descent to a safe landing speed. The whole escapade would take about three minutes.

Knievel played up the danger of his stunt for all it was worth. He told reporters he would make it... "if the heater doesn't

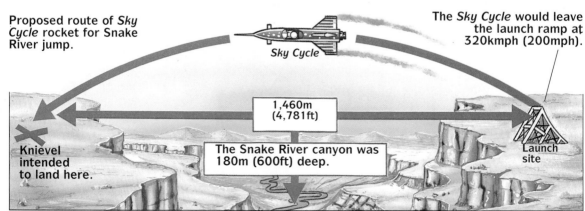

Proposed route of *Sky Cycle* rocket for Snake River jump.

Sky Cycle

The *Sky Cycle* would leave the launch ramp at 320kmph (200mph).

1,460m (4,781ft)

The Snake River canyon was 180m (600ft) deep.

Knievel intended to land here.

Launch site

blow up and scald me to death, if the *Sky Cycle* goes straight up and doesn't flip over backward, if I reach 3,000ft, if the parachute opens and if I don't hit the canyon wall at 300mph."

The date was set – September 8, 1974. Word went out and within weeks the audacious stunt had captured the imagination of newspaper editors throughout the world. Fifteen different businesses invested in it. There would be toys, T-shirts, records, even statuettes ($450 in bronze, $20,000 in silver, $140,000 in gold).

As the date drew near, 50,000 spectators gathered at the Snake River site, paying $25 a ticket. Most lucrative of all was the plan to broadcast the action to several million paying customers in theatres throughout the world.

Hero or zero?

Opinion on Knievel was sharply divided. To his thousands of fans he was "the last gladiator", shaking a defiant fist at the fiery holocaust or watery grave that awaited. Many believed he was actually going to die. According to his publicity men, his escapade would most likely "leave behind the richest widow in America".

But to others the stunt was a con, and the danger had been exaggerated beyond all reason. A bright teenager, they said, could have calculated the rocket's flight path and concluded that Knievel would land perfectly safely. One

cynic, regarding the surly mob of desperado bikers who made up most of the Snake River spectators, speculated that the crowd was more dangerous than the *Sky Cycle*.

Even the man himself was unsure. "I don't know if I'm an athlete, a daredevil, a promoter, a hoax, or just a nut".

So it was, on the afternoon of September 8, 1974, that Evel Knievel mounted his

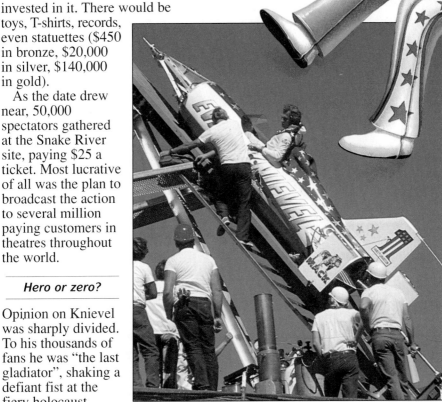

Knievel doll, complete with gold-topped cane. Publicity from the Snake River jump led to sales of millions of toys such as this.

Festooned with sponsors' logos, the million dollar *Sky Cycle* is prepared for liftoff. Two previous, unmanned flights ended in disaster.

Sky Cycle, and launched himself into the air. But his flight was to be less than glorious. As the rocket sped from the 58° ramp, a parachute accidentally opened right in the way of its steam-powered thruster.

The flight of the *Sky Cycle* was now fatally flawed and it lurched into the canyon,

parachute billowing behind. Knievel struggled to escape his tiny cockpit, but could not free himself in time to make his own parachute jump to safety. The *Sky Cycle* grazed the craggy wall of the canyon, and then deposited the hapless stunt man in the Snake River.

Knievel, swiftly rescued by boat and helicopter, appeared shaken but uninjured. His stunt had turned out to be hair-raisingly dangerous after all. However, disappointed by his unspectacular performance, sections of the crowd promptly rioted. They attempted to storm the press enclosure and were beaten off by policemen.

But injured pride was a small price to pay. With a guaranteed minimum fee of $5,500,000, or 60 per cent of all takings, Knievel's final performance had blossomed into an awesome retirement pay off.

Marooned in a polar wilderness

With a screeching and groaning that would have done justice to a dying mammoth, the *Endurance* finally began to break up. Crushed for months by massive sheets of pack ice, the ship was slowly sinking. Even her hardened hull (made from greenheart, a wood heavier than iron) could not withstand such tremendous pressure.

The Trans-Antarctic Expedition

Watching in numb resignation were the 29 men of Ernest Shackleton's Trans-Antarctic Expedition. This hand-picked mixture of seamen, scientists and craftsmen was accompanied by 70 dogs, a cat and a stowaway – 18-year-old Canadian Percy Blackboro. When discovered, Shackleton had told him "If anyone has to be eaten, you'll be the first."

They had intended to spend 1914-15 attempting the first crossing of the Antarctic. Now, in November, 1915, they were stranded, 1,900km (1,200 miles) from the nearest human beings, in one of the most hostile places on Earth.

Endurance, **trapped in ice. In other boats, caught in similar conditions, crews had gone mad or squabbled violently. Shackleton ensured his men were well occupied as they waited for the ice to melt.**

The *Endurance* had sailed from London. When they reached Antarctic waters, icebergs soon surrounded the ship. As they passed gingerly through, Shackleton described their unearthly environment as

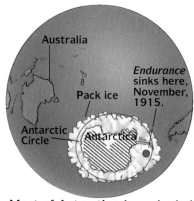

Most of Antarctica (see shaded area) was unexplored at the time of Shackleton's expedition.

"a gigantic and interminable jigsaw". But shortly after crossing the Antarctic Circle the ice closed in and packed itself tightly around them. Soon they could move neither forward nor backward, and there they stayed for nine months, waiting for the ice to clear.

The expedition coped with the waiting, the cold and the interminable darkness of an Antarctic winter with remarkable cheerfulness. Shackleton, called "the Boss" by the crew, kept them busy organizing dog training, soccer and hockey matches, party games and lectures. The men even carved blocks of ice into elaborate, beautiful dog kennels. In anticipation of such delays, the *Endurance* had also been equipped with an ample library.

Ocean Camp

But now the ship had sunk, and the men made a camp on the ice. Surrounded by an untidy mixture of three lifeboats, salvaged equipment and supplies,

Sir Ernest Shackleton was a professional adventurer. When not exploring, he made a living writing books and giving lectures about his expeditions.

they christened their new home "Ocean Camp". Here Shackleton gathered his companions around him. They were too far from civilization to be rescued, he told them. If they were to survive, drastic measures were called for.

Their only option, he said, was to haul the lifeboats through the ice to the open sea, and then sail 1,300km (800 miles) back to South Georgia – the nearest inhabited island. Each man could only bring 1kg (2lbs) of personal possessions, and would have to leave most of his belongings behind.

To emphasize this point, Shackleton threw to the ground his watch and chain, and a pocketful of gold coins. Then, to everyone's amazement, a Bible the Queen of England had given him at the start of the voyage was also discarded.

Banjo sing-along

Men were allowed to keep their diaries. Leonard Hussey, the expedition meteorologist, was told to keep his banjo – a sing-along was always good for morale. A sleeping bag, metal cup, knife, spoon and the heavy clothes they stood in, were the only other possessions they were allowed to take.

Food supplies were so limited that there would not be enough for both the members of the expedition and their animals. Some of the dogs, and the ship's cat, were reluctantly shot. It was kinder than letting them starve to death.

By the time they were ready to set off on their trek, it was almost Christmas and well into the Antarctic summer. (In the northern and southern

Endurance **sinks into the ice, November, 1915.**

hemispheres, seasons occur at opposite times of the year.) Shackleton, impatient to depart, designated December 22, the day before their leaving, to be Christmas Day.

Christmas feast

Despite the shortages, this was celebrated with a feast of ham, sausage, stewed hare, pickle and peaches. The men, fortified and in good spirits, loaded the boats

Shackleton's men discarded anything that was not essential for their trip back home.

and sleighs and began towing toward the sea.

Hauling their loads was hot, exhausting work, so they stumbled on in the below-zero cool of the night. In the first five days they managed only 14km (9 miles) and morale slumped alarmingly. Illness swept through the party. More dogs had to be shot. Arguments broke out and Shackleton had to remind mutinous men that their pay, which they would receive in a lump sum at the end of the expedition, could be stopped.

Three-month drift

Shackleton decided their best hope was to make another camp, and drift north on the shifting ice. This they did for three months, and food and fuel supplies dwindled alarmingly.

Then, one morning, a huge leopard seal poked its head out of a crack in the ice and stared at Seaman Thomas McLeod. Both eyed the other as a potential meal, but McLeod was shrewder.

He began flapping his arms like a penguin – the seal's main prey – and, as the beast

Hauling one of the lifeboats, (the *James Caird**) to the sea. December, 1915.

lumbered out of the ice and after him, it was briskly shot. A catch as substantial as this provided the expedition with enough seal meat to allay fears of starvation and plenty of blubber to burn in their stoves.

The open ocean

At last, in early April, 1916, they reached open ocean and the three lifeboats were put to sea. Elephant Island was the nearest land, and it was here they headed. The boats were small, crammed with men and supplies, and open to the terrible weather. At night, if they slept in the boats, schools of killer whales would surround them. If they stopped to make camp on an ice floe, sleeping men would plunge through cracks into the freezing sea and have to scramble out before the ice closed above them.

Elephant Island

Seven days of unrelenting misery and constant bailing passed before the snow covered peaks of Elephant Island loomed before them. The expedition were still 1,100km (700 miles) away from the nearest inhabited land, but the men were deliriously happy to have survived such an appalling journey. It was their first time on solid ground for nearly one and a half years.

This narrow, 37km (23 miles) long island was bare rock. There were no trees, but there were plenty of birds and elephant seals to eat. As they lacked any other shelter, the two smaller boats were turned upside down and made into huts.

Recruiting a crew

This was Shackleton's third trip to the Antarctic. Although explorers had reached the South Pole, no one had yet crossed the continent, and that was the intention of this expedition. Once his plans became known, 5,000 letters of application flooded into Shackleton's central London headquarters in Burlington Street. He had already decided on some of the key members, but the rest of the crew he picked on instinct, often taking only seconds to hire complete strangers.

Good teeth and temper

Expedition scientist Reginald James was asked if his teeth were good, if he had a good temper and if he could sing. When he looked shocked at this question, Shackleton explained he wanted someone who could "shout a bit with the boys". On a trip such as this, getting along with other people was just as important as scientific expertise.

Strange dream

Endurance's captain Frank Worsley joined the team after a strange dream. "One night I dreamed that Burlington Street was full of ice blocks and that I was navigating a ship along it." Next morning he went to Burlington Street where a sign reading "Imperial Trans-Antarctic Expedition" caught his eye. Worsley recalled "Shackleton was there, and the moment I set eyes on him I knew he was a man with whom I would be proud to work."

Boat-hut home for 135 days

Two lifeboats provided shelter on Elephant Island.

An improvised stove provided a little heat.

The boats were placed on stones and sealed with moss and fabric.

Window, made with glass from the *Endurance's* chronometer.

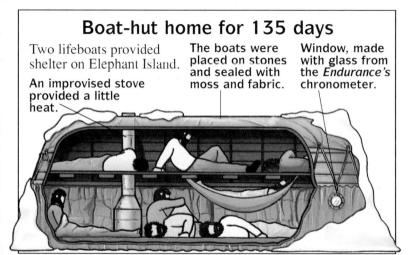

Back to sea

No one would find them on Elephant Island, it was too remote, but Shackleton was wary of putting his vulnerable fleet to sea again. He decided to take the biggest boat, the *James Caird*, and a small crew, and return to sea. The rest of his expedition would wait on the island for rescue.

One of Shackleton's greatest talents as a leader was his ability to pick the right people for a job, and for this perilous trip he chose a mixture of the most able and most troublesome men. The latter he took to save the patience of those who would have to endure a depressingly long wait on Elephant Island.

To South Georgia

The *James Caird* and its crew of six set out to travel 1,125km (700 miles) to South Georgia, where there were several whaling stations. Once again they had to battle through blizzards and gales. Constantly soaked and freezing, they suffered from raging thirst as salt water had contaminated their water supply.

After 17 days at sea they reached South Georgia. Just off the coast a terrible gale ripped away their rudder and they were washed up on the opposite side of the island to the whaling stations.

South Georgia was long and narrow, like Elephant Island, but it was also mountainous. As the boat was no longer fit to sail, and the walk around the coast was over 240km (150 miles), they would have to risk their lives again to cross these uncharted mountains.

Into the unknown

On May 19, 1916, taking only 15m (50ft) of rope and a carpenter's axe, Shackleton, *Endurance's* captain Frank Worsley and officer Thomas Crean began their climb into the unknown. Two men too weak to go on were left behind, with a third to look after them.

Shackleton and his two companions pressed on, up and down for two days, one time tobogganing down a steep ice slope on their coiled-up rope, another time climbing down a waterfall. Once, when they stopped to rest, Shackleton let the other two sleep for five minutes, and then woke them, telling them half an hour had passed by.

Stromness

On May 20, at 7:00am, the men heard a factory whistle at Stromness whaling station. For the first time since December 1914, here was evidence that other human beings were close by.

Dreaming of vegetables

Although the expedition never did run out of food, everyone became desperately weary of their diet of meat. During the day they would huddle around a blubber stove and fantasize aloud about puddings and pastries. At night they dreamed of salads and omelettes.

Adelie penguins were their staple diet. They were easy to catch, but too small to provide much nourishment.

Occasionally a leopard seal was caught. Although its meat was unappetizing, a seal provided enough blubber (fat) for two weeks' cooking fuel. The one that chased Thomas McLeod had 50 undigested fish in its stomach, which made a welcome change from seal and penguin meat.

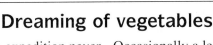

As they walked toward the factory, two boys, terrified by these ragged apparitions, ran away screaming. Shackleton asked to be taken to the home of factory manager Thoralf Sørlle, whom he knew well. When he opened the door, Sørlle gawped at them in astonishment and said "Who the hell are you?" Like everyone at Grytviken, he had assumed that the *Endurance* had been lost with all aboard. When Shackleton told him, Sørlle was moved to tears.

A hot bath and a hearty meal was all Shackleton's party needed before they set out to rescue their stranded companions. The men on the other side of South Georgia were picked up the next day, but Elephant Island was more difficult to reach. It was 14 frustrating weeks before the Trans-

Antarctic Expedition was finally reunited. Severe ice, fog and violent storms thwarted several rescue attempts.

Shackleton sailed out on a relief ship on May 23, but ice blocked his route. A second attempt to reach the island was thwarted by fog. On the third attempt, rough weather forced them to turn back.

The long journey back to civilization

Arrive Elephant Island, April 15.

James Caird sails to South Georgia.

Route to open sea.

Lifeboats take to sea. April 9, 1916.

Arrive May 10.

Endurance sinks. Camp set up. November, 1915.

South Georgia

Stromness whaling station

Weddell Sea

0   400 km
0   250 miles

The stranded expedition fought their way to Elephant Island. From here Shackleton and five others reached South Georgia. The rest of the men were rescued in August, 1916 (below).

Rescue at last

Shackleton and his relief ship finally reached Elephant Island on August 30, 1916. A small boat was dispatched toward the shore and Shackleton, standing on its bow, anxiously counted the 22 men he had left behind.

They were all there. The four-month wait had been a tedious ordeal, best summed up in a diary entry by one of *Endurance*'s officers, Lionel Greenstreet: "So passes another goddam rotten day." Although the men had suffered from infections and boils, the only real casualty of the two-year adventure had been the ship's stowaway, Percy Blackboro. He had lost the toes of his left foot to frostbite. Shackleton had managed, through good judgment and great leadership, to bring his entire expedition back to civilization alive.

Film crew in lava inferno

F ew things in nature match the forbidding power of a smoking volcano, threatening to unleash massive destruction with a terrifying roar and rumble. Its sinister might has become a potent symbol for movie makers. During the filming of *Sliver* in 1992, director Phillip Noyce despatched Hollywood film cameramen Michael Benson, 42, and Chris Duddy, 31, to Pu'u O'o (pronounced POO oo OH oo) in Hawaii's Volcanoes National Park, to capture a steaming volcano in action.

Madame Pele

Benson, a veteran of films such as *Patriot Games* and *Terminator II*, was a seasoned professional. He was also superstitious. Local folklore told of a fearsome goddess, named Madame Pele, who lurked within the volcano's fiery cone. She was reputed to be very fond of gin, so, as a gesture of goodwill, the crew brought a bottle with them to throw into the crater, hoping to ensure their safety and good weather for filming.

On the morning of Saturday, November 21, they hired pilot Craig Hosking, 34, and his Bell Jet Ranger helicopter, and flew from Hilo Bay airfield to Pu'u O'o. The weather was damp and foggy, and showed little sign of clearing as they approached the ash-strewn summit. Below, a steaming, bubbling cauldron lurked within a

Hawaiian carving of Madame Pele.

jagged, disfigured peak. Corrosive, choking gases, venting from the glowing lava pits inside the massive crater, cast thick clouds over the volcano, making it almost impossible to see.

Even in the relative comfort and safety of the helicopter, the fumes caught in the men's throats. As they made their first pass over the rim, Benson lobbed the gin bottle into the crater.

Engine trouble

Gaps in the clouds came and went, allowing Benson and Duddy to shoot some film. But as they prepared to make a final flight over before returning home, the helicopter engine began to splutter.

Hosking, wide-eyed with alarm, wrestled with the controls, desperate to avoid having to make a landing inside the steaming crater.

But he was fighting a losing battle and the craft was heading straight over the rim. Narrowly missing a deep pool of glowing lava in the middle of the crater, he tried to direct the stricken helicopter to a flat rock ledge.

Crash landing

As they pitched and rolled, the rotor hit the ground and shattered. The craft dropped with a sickening thud and broke in half. Benson, Duddy and Hosking scrambled out, battered but

uninjured, and found themselves in a hellish environment.

Although they were fortunate enough to have landed on a thin crust of solid rock, the heat of the molten lava beneath penetrated through their boots. An intense and constant roar filled their ears as pools of lava bubbled and boiled, and steam hissed and spluttered from cracks in the ground. Clouds of acrid gas drifted by and the men could barely see their hands in front of their faces.

No chance of rescue

Within the shattered cockpit, the radio was dead. There was no chance of immediate rescue – they were not expected back for another hour. The obvious option was to head for the rim, 50m (150ft) above. The rocky surroundings they scrambled through regularly gave way to deep ash and crumbling stone, and they sank knee-deep in hot black soot.

The camera crew threw a bottle of gin into the volcano as a goodwill offering.

After about 15 minutes the three had climbed halfway up the slope to the top, but could go no higher. The rock ahead rose to 45°, then jutted into an overhanging rim that looked almost impassable.

Radio repair

It seemed impossible to get out without assistance, but all three knew no one would see them in the crater. Hosking had one reckless idea – he would go back to the helicopter and try to repair the radio.

Benson tried to persuade him not to return, since the craft was enveloped in poisonous, choking fumes. But Hosking knew he had no option. Wrapping his shirt around his face to keep out the worst of the acrid air, he returned to the helicopter.

Help on the way

Hosking could only work at the radio for short bursts, emerging occasionally to climb to a clearer spot and breathe some fresher air. But he managed to take a film camera battery and hook it to the radio, and after a grim hour he was able to fix it. An SOS call soon caught the attention of colleagues back at his base. Within an hour, pilot Don Shearer, who had often worked on rescue missions in the Hawaii area, was flying over the volcano. Shearer, in radio contact with Hosking, reported that he could see nothing in the smoking crater. Hosking would have to guide him in.

Peering blindly into the swirling smoke, Hosking could now faintly hear the dull thrubbing of rotor blades, and was able to bring Sheerer down close by. As the craft hovered a couple of feet above the ground, Hosking leaped inside,

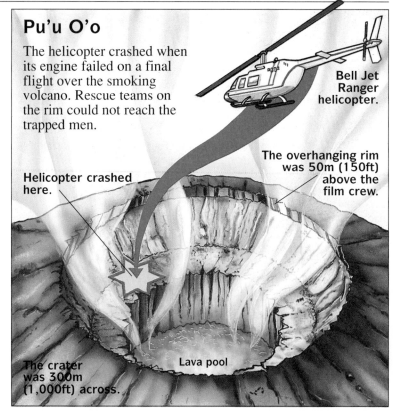

Pu'u O'o

The helicopter crashed when its engine failed on a final flight over the smoking volcano. Rescue teams on the rim could not reach the trapped men.

Bell Jet Ranger helicopter.

Helicopter crashed here.

The overhanging rim was 50m (150ft) above the film crew.

The crater was 300m (1,000ft) across.

Lava pool

and watched the clouds of smoke swirl away beneath him as the helicopter lifted him away to safety.

One out

One man at least had escaped the clutches of Madame Pele, but Benson and Duddy were still awaiting rescue, crouching on a ledge, halfway up the crater. They had noticed the helicopter's arrival and were distressed to hear its engines recede into the distance.

But above them, help had arrived from another quarter. Hosking's radio SOS had also been picked up by the local National Park rangers. Two rangers had climbed to the tip of the rim, and were trying to spot the survivors. So deadly was the atmosphere around the volcano summit that the rangers had to wear gas masks, and acidic fumes corroded their climbing ropes.

Benson and Duddy could hear faint shouts from their would-be rescuers above the roar of the lava pits. Waving frantically, they shouted themselves hoarse. But the cloudy fumes were too thick, and their muffled voices echoed around the rim, making it impossible for them to be located.

The rangers threw down ropes in the vague hope that one would land near the trapped men, but this was unsuccessful. Darkness fell, and the rescuers gave up, intending to return the next morning.

Night brought torrential rain and the next day the weather was even rougher. Don Shearer was no longer able to help because his helicopter had been damaged by corrosive fumes when he rescued Hosking and it was now unsafe to fly. On the rim of the crater, the rangers could hardly see 3m (10ft) in front of them.

The day wore on and Benson

and Duddy faced another night in the crater, to be baked by glowing lava, and frozen by lashing rain. Choked by fumes, their eyes streaming, the two had only their shirts to wrap around their faces to protect them from the poisonous surroundings.

Desperate move

By mid-afternoon on the second day in the crater, Duddy could take no more. Maybe there was another way out? Whatever happened, trying to escape was better than sitting there suffocating. Benson, who was older, and not so confident of his climbing ability, decided to stay where he was.

Duddy's gamble paid off. After an exhausting climb through crumbling rock and sooty gravel, he eventually made it to the top, and was rescued by Park rangers. He shouted down to Benson, but his voice was lost in the huge, hollow cauldron.

Night supplies

Night was now falling and, for want of any better plan of action, the rangers tossed food and water packets into the rim, hoping that Benson might stumble on one.

But the well-meaning gesture only brought him more misery. Seeing one of the packages fall through the mist, he thought it was Duddy falling to his death, and was overwhelmed by guilt for bringing his crew here at all.

Again, it rained for most of the night and Benson, who had not found any of the packets tossed to him, was weakening fast. Breathing was now a painful effort. His mouth was so dry he could no longer call for help, and the fumes were causing him to hallucinate.

He battled with a raging thirst, catching rain in the face of his camera light meter, and drinking a mouthful at a time.

But help was on its way from yet another quarter. Overnight, Benson's colleagues had managed to contact helicopter pilot Tom Hauptman, famed for his daring rescues. Soon after first light Hauptman flew over the crater rim, and for the first time, through a temporary gap in the clouds, he managed to spot Benson, who waved frantically back.

Net rescue

Hauptman's helicopter was equipped with a large net, and this was dangled down. It was like fishing in a muddy pool, for Hauptman could only guess where Benson was, as the clouds obscured his view. Twice the net went down, and twice it came out empty. But on the third attempt it landed right in front of the ailing cameraman. He saw his chance and lunged into it. Intense relief flooded through him as the helicopter pulled away from the crater – he was safe at last.

Benson drank the rainwater that collected in a light meter, to quench his thirst.

World record

The helicopter landed nearby, and Benson was bundled into an ambulance and rushed to Hawaii's Hilo hospital. The cameraman had been exposed to the volcano's poisonous fumes for over 48 hours. He had serious damage to his lungs, but was able to make a full recovery. Duddy and Hosking were lucky enough to escape with fairly minor injuries.

Benson might have taken some comfort from the fact that the rangers who rescued him were convinced that he had set a world record for the length of time anyone had managed to survive inside an active volcano.

Michael Benson, surrounded by medical personnel, after his dramatic rescue from Pu'u O'o.

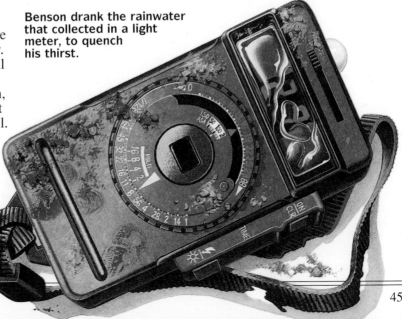

Plenty of fish in sea, says scientist

The Fonvieille quayside was packed that bright May afternoon in 1952. The crowd's attention focused on two men busily preparing an inflatable dinghy, *L'Hérétique,* for an extraordinary journey. A young French doctor, Alain Bombard, and his English navigator, Jack Palmer, planned to take their rubber boat on a trial run through the Mediterranean and then sail across the Atlantic.

To take this tiny boat on such a voyage was foolhardy enough, but Bombard and Palmer intended to live entirely on what they caught on the journey. They had supplies of food and drink, but these were sealed, and only intended for a life-or-death emergency. Bombard had an untried theory which he was burning to prove: that all the water and food a castaway needed to survive was in the sea around him.

Doctor Bombard. His concern for castaways prompted a daring solo Atlantic crossing.

Shipwreck concern

Doctor Bombard's concern for castaways began when he worked in a hospital near the coast and was called out to attend to shipwreck victims. He discovered that over 200,000 people died in shipwrecks every year. Of that number, 50,000 made it to lifeboats, but 90 per cent of these survivors died within three days.

Bombard's sea diet

A healthy diet needs a mixture of particular kinds of food. Bombard believed that the sea could provide almost all of them.

Healthy diet	Sea diet
Protein (such as meat, milk, cheese).	Fish and plankton* are rich in protein.
Fat (such as oil and butter).	Fish are rich in fat.
Carbohydrates (such as bread and potatoes.)	Plankton contain a few carbohydrates.
Vitamins and minerals (found in fruit and vegetables, for example).	Fish, plankton and sea water contain essential vitamins and minerals.
Water. Essential to life. Most people will die after three days without a drink.	Fish are between 58-82 percent water. Sea water too can be drunk in small amounts.

His sea diet was low on carbohydrates, but if the body has the right amount of water, protein and fat, it can make its own carbohydrates.

Most, it was supposed, died of exhaustion and despair.

Bombard felt that if castaways knew how to live off the resources of the sea, then their chances of survival would be increased dramatically.

He decided to study this idea in detail, and was provided with facilities and support at the Museum of Oceanography in Monaco. Here he studied case histories of previous successful castaways (including the *Bounty* survivors, see p. 13-17), and made detailed research into human nutritional needs and the type of nutrition provided by the sea.

Saltwater drink

Bombard's findings showed that there would be enough nutriment in the sea to sustain a castaway. His most controversial theory was that it was possible to drink sea water. He knew it caused serious damage to the kidneys, but argued that if a castaway only drank one litre (1.5 pints) a day, for no longer than five days, his health would not suffer. It was most important to drink sea water immediately, however, rather than wait until the body became dehydrated. Within five days, suggested Bombard, the castaway would then be able to find water from other sources such as rain and fish.

The voyage begins

So, on May 26, 1952, Doctor Bombard and his English companion set off to prove to the world that his theories were correct. Although he had many eminent supporters, the Press were quick to dismiss him as an eccentric and poured scorn on the voyage.

However, the trial run across the Mediterranean was encouraging. They drank salt water and lived. They caught enough fish to ward off starvation. The boat was subjected to some frightening storms, but did not sink.

After 14 days, *L'Hérétique* landed at Minorca, the first island on their route. They had proved it was possible to survive perfectly well. Anxious not to waste any more time and effort before the real test of the Atlantic Ocean, they packed their equipment and headed for Tangiers by ocean liner.

Before they faced the Atlantic, Bombard decided he needed a new boat and flew to Paris to arrange this. Rubber dinghies wear out and it was best to make the ocean crossing with a new one. He returned with an identical model, which he christened with the same name.

Delays were inevitable and Jack Palmer began to lose heart. Bombard, sensing his reluctance, and afraid they no longer had a common purpose, decided he would have to make the voyage on his own.

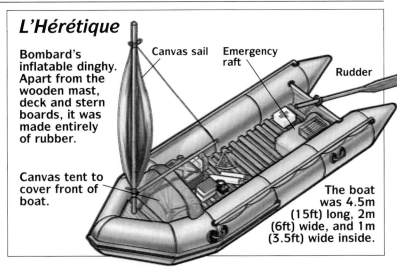

L'Hérétique

Bombard's inflatable dinghy. Apart from the wooden mast, deck and stern boards, it was made entirely of rubber.

Canvas sail

Emergency raft

Rudder

Canvas tent to cover front of boat.

The boat was 4.5m (15ft) long, 2m (6ft) wide, and 1m (3.5ft) wide inside.

Atlantic odyssey

On August 14, Bombard sailed into the Atlantic Ocean alone. He realized at once that this voyage would be different from the trial run. Here, time was measured in weeks not days, and distances by thousands rather than tens of miles.

Going alone was an act of extraordinary courage. Palmer was an expert navigator and Bombard now had to acquire his ex-partner's skills. He had packed navigation books and charts for the voyage, and these he pored over, learning as quickly as he could.

Following a brief stopover in Casablanca, after a week at sea, he set out for the Canary Islands. Again, food was no problem, the coastal waters of the Atlantic were rich in fish, but his log betrayed his real problems.

Fishing techniques

Fish are an essential ingredient in the castaway's diet so it is vital to be able to catch them. A simple line and hook, or harpoon, are all a castaway needs. Bombard also offered these suggestions.
• Night time is the best time to catch fish and plankton. Both come closer to the surface after dark and are easier to catch.
• A straining cloth, folded into a net, and attached to a 20m (60ft) line, can be used to catch plankton.

"Sunday, August 24 ...Use of sextant becoming more complicated, having doubts about this longitude business."
"Thursday, August 28... Horribly alone. Nothing in sight. Complete novice as navigator. Do not know where I am, but only suppose I do."

Canary stopover

By September 3, Bombard reached the Canary Islands, 11 days after leaving Casablanca. Here he found out that his wife Ginette had given birth to a baby girl, Natalie, so he flew back to Paris to see her.

Although the Press were quick to ridicule his efforts, and even Jack Palmer was now describing the final and longest leg of the journey as "suicidal madness", Bombard returned to the Canaries with his wife's blessing, determined to complete his voyage.

Before he set off again, he installed a radio receiver in *L'Hérétique*. He had missed Palmer very much and badly needed some human company, even if it was only a voice on the radio.

His voyage resumed on October 19. Heading west, the nearest land was now the islands of the Caribbean.

This was 6,000km (3,750 miles) away, and Bombard hoped to get there in 40 days. If anything went wrong he had no way of calling for help.

The monotony of the voyage was broken by violent storms, when Bombard had to bail constantly to stop his boat from becoming swamped. In a storm he had one clear philosophy which ensured his survival. "Be more obstinate than the sea, and you will win."

Five days out from the Canaries, disaster struck. His sail was torn in half by the wind and Bombard spent a day carefully sewing it back together. For the rest of the voyage he worried constantly that it would rip again.

Failure and success

As the voyage progressed, his morale dropped. Soaked, shivering, encrusted with salt, Bombard spent long nights waiting wearily for the sun to rise and offer him a little comfort. Although he did not know it, he began to make serious errors of navigation.

But he also had some successes. Trying to use as much makeshift equipment as

Fishing, repairing the boat and keeping a detailed log took up most of Bombard's day. To relax he read books or music scores.

he could (he reasoned that a castaway would not have proper fishing equipment) Bombard made a useful harpoon with a knife and oar. When he caught a dorado fish, he fashioned a hook from a bone found behind its gills. He caught plenty of fish with this crude equipment.

His greatest trials came from

the sheer, unrelenting hostility of his environment. Bombard tried to make his circumstances as close to those of a real castaway as possible. He wore only everyday clothes (again reasoning that a castaway would not have protective clothing) and his body soon began to suffer the effects of prolonged exposure to constant

Bombard's busy day

Despair is quick to settle on a castaway because his unchanging existence is so soul-destroying. Bombard strove to bring a clear, disciplined structure to his day. His philosophy was that castaways should remain masters of events, rather than just react to them. He rose with the dawn and slept at dusk, and took careful records of his health and diet.

Morning
- **Wake at dawn. Clear flying fish which have landed on *L'Hérétique* overnight. Eat two largest for breakfast.**
- **Fish for one hour. Divide haul into lunch and supper.**
- **Inspect boat for one hour. Ensure nothing is scraping on rubber skin. Run fingers over entire surface, feeling for leaks. Make repairs.**
- **Exercise for half an hour.**
- **Catch two spoonfuls of plankton. This is rich in vitamin C, vital for keeping scurvy* at bay.**
- **12:00 noon. Take position with sextant.**

Afternoon
- Eat lunch.
- Write log.
- 2:00pm. medical check up. Record details of temperature, blood pressure, condition of skin, hair and nails, morale, memory, reflexes.
- Relax. Read books and music scores.

Evening
- Evening medical.
- Write log.
- Eat supper.

Dusk
- Listen to radio.
- Go to sleep.

20

*Scurvy – a disease which harms skin, teeth and blood.

damp, cold and salt water. Bombard's diet kept hunger and thirst at bay. He found he could drink enough water by cutting slits in the flanks of fish and sucking the juice. But the diet was not enough to keep him healthy. He lost weight, and his body became covered in red sores and rashes. Sitting and lying down became uncomfortable. Fingernails and toenails dropped off. He began to crave the food his body needed – fruit and vegetables – and he longed for a huge glass of ice-cold beer.

Shark shock

One warm night he discovered he could attract shoals of fish by shining a flashlight into the sea. As he amused himself moving the beam and watching the fish dart after it, a huge shark, ferocious teeth flashing, lunged out of the water. Thrashing around the boat, it soaked him to the skin and butted the rubber keel with its sandpapery snout. Bombard sat stock-still, almost too terrified to breathe, until the monster lost interest and left.

Although he was attacked by several other sharks, and a swordfish, he usually took comfort from the sea creatures he encountered. One dolphin shoal stayed with him for days. When his boat slowed down in a low wind, they would smack the floats with their tails, as if to hurry him along.

Lost at sea

After 11 days at sea, Bombard was convinced he had completed a quarter of the journey. But he had covered far less than that and was still well to the north of the Cape Verde Islands. Bombard became increasingly baffled by his sextant sightings, and even began to think his compass was playing tricks on him. He did not seem to be where he thought he was at all.

His sense of isolation deepened as the batteries of his radio faded. Continuous storms and rain tormented him, and his log entries show a man in deep depression. The low, grey sky, he recalled, "seemed about to crush me." When the weather turned, and the sky, cleared he was baked rather than frozen.

The night offered no refuge from his despair. Fear of shark or swordfish attack, or of being swamped by a huge wave, kept him wide awake. On November 27, after 40 days at sea, his log reads "I have had enough". By December 6 his health had deteriorated so much that he wrote his will. An upset stomach, and the dehydration this caused, had exhausted him.

The flapping sail irritated him unbearably and he began to feel persecuted by the objects on the boat. When writing his log, he would feel that his pencil had deliberately hidden itself when he wanted to use it.

Arakaka arrives

But on December 9, he spotted a large cargo ship heading straight for him. He grabbed his heliograph*, and began to flash at the bridge, and soon he was being helped on board the British vessel *Arakaka*. The news that he was 960km (600 miles) farther east than he thought came as a bitter blow, and Bombard almost gave up then and there. But he wanted to convince his critics, especially the Press, that his theories were correct. Only a complete voyage across the Atlantic would satisfy them.

A freshwater shower, a small meal, new batteries for his radio and a new set of books to navigate by, were all provided by the helpful crew. Greatly encouraged, and reassured that his wife would know he was safe, Bombard continued on his journey.

Nearly there

For 12 more days he battled against the Atlantic. Aside from the usual problems, his boat had now started to deteriorate. Water was seeping in through the bottom and Bombard spent much of the rest of the voyage bailing.

The flashes of a lighthouse indicated that the end was near, and by dawn the next day the coast of Barbados was in sight. Local fishermen helped him ashore, but were eager to grab as much of his supplies and equipment as they could lay their hands on.

For a few horrible moments Bombard thought they would seize his sealed food and water supplies, destroying the sole proof that he had survived only on what the sea had provided. Fortunately, a policeman arrived to restore order. He took Bombard to the local police station, and gave him tea and bread and butter. It seemed a strange way to celebrate after a total of 65 continuous days at sea.

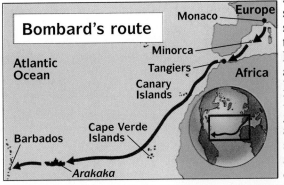

Bombard's route

Europe
Monaco
Minorca
Tangiers
Africa
Atlantic Ocean
Canary Islands
Cape Verde Islands
Barbados
Arakaka

*Communications instrument which reflects the Sun's rays with a mirror.

49

Terror in the skies

Griffiths' iron grip

On a crisp December morning in 1942, a Boston bomber took off from Wayzata airfield, Minnesota, USA. Climbing into a cloudless sky were American test pilot Sid Gerow, 29, and Canadian test observer Harry Griffiths, 20. Their job was to give the factory-fresh aircraft a thorough checking before it flew the Atlantic to serve in World War Two.

When the plane reached 2,100m (7,000ft) Gerow began to test the controls and engines, while Griffiths monitored the instrument panel. There were no problems and all that remained to be inspected was the bombsight* in the forward section. Griffiths climbed inside the perspex nose of the plane and lay on his stomach.

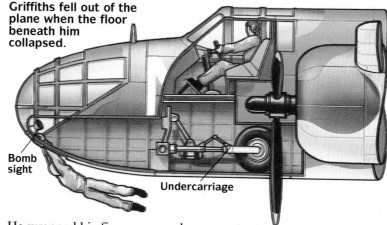

Griffiths fell out of the plane when the floor beneath him collapsed.

Bomb sight

Undercarriage

Bottom falls out of world

As he peered into the sight, which was set at the very tip of the nose, Griffiths felt the floor beneath give way. The forward entry hatch, which he had been lying on, had fallen off.

Instinctively he gripped the bombsight with both hands, but an immense gust of freezing air sucked him out of the aircraft. With the wind roaring in his ears, he found himself halfway out of the plane, legs and lower body pressed against the fuselage.

Griffiths' fingers quickly lost their grip on the polished metal instrument. As his head slipped out of the plane, he clutched desperately at the wooden fitting beneath the sight. The surrounding temperature was -25°C (-13°F) and fierce cold gnawed at his battered body.

Harry Griffiths was small, but he was immensely strong.

He wrapped his fingers around the wooden fitting and held on with a vice-like grip. Buffeted mercilessly by the plane's turbulent slipstream, few other men could have clung to such a precarious niche.

But cling he did, for he had no other option. He called feebly for help, but his cries were snatched away by the fierce wind. Very soon, his grip would weaken, and he would fall to his death.

Help at hand?

In the cockpit above the open hatch, Sid Gerow was all too aware of what had happened. Cold air had billowed into the plane, and a fierce wind howled around his boots. Griffiths had not answered his urgent enquiries, but Gerow imagined he could hear his comrade's faint shouts for help.

But, if Griffiths was still alive, there was precious little the pilot could do for him. He could not leave the controls, for without him the plane would plummet to the ground. He could not land – if he lowered the undercarriage, the front wheel would dislodge his dangling companion. Gerow wracked his brains, desperate for something, anything, to

save Griffiths' life. As he flew on, the sun caught in the frozen waters of Lake St. Louis 2,100m (7,000ft) below, momentarily dazzling him. Inspiration struck. Gerow quickly dived, approaching the lake as low and as slowly as he dared. Anyone falling from a speeding plane onto earth or water would surely die. But ice... maybe that would be different?

Ice crash landing

Beneath the plane Griffiths understood at once what he needed to do. As the ice raced beneath him at over 160kmph (100mph) he released his grip. For a brief moment he glided above the surface, then hit the ice with a sickening thud, shooting along the frozen surface for 1km (half a mile).

Circling above, Gerow watched his partner slowly drift to a halt. He lay quite still, but then, miraculously, hauled himself to his feet and walked toward the shore.

Harry Griffiths was rushed to hospital and the next eight days of his life were a total blank. But apart from severe bruising, and mild frostbite, he had survived his extraordinary ordeal without serious injury.

*Instrument in aircraft for aiming bombs.

Captain Lancaster's window exit

Captain Lancaster

It was a routine trip for Captain Timothy Lancaster and copilot Alastair Atchison, flying a British Airways BAC 1-11 from Birmingham, England, to Malaga, Spain, on June 8, 1990. But as the plane reached 7,000m (23,000ft), a front window panel, which had just been refitted, blew off.

Air inside the cabin was sucked out with tremendous force, taking stray papers, flight routes, jackets and cups with it. Lancaster too was hauled from his seat into the gaping hole. As he shot out, his leg struck the flight controls, and the plane banked alarmingly, terrifying the passengers. At that very moment, steward Nigel Ogden had been serving hot drinks to the crew, and made a frantic grab for the pilot's legs. Steward John Heward also rushed to the cabin and, strapping himself into Lancaster's seat, he held on to both Ogden and the pilot.

Lancaster, pinned to the top of the plane by an 800kmph (500mph) slipstream, struggled desperately for breath. His shirt had been ripped off and the temperature outside was -25°C (-13°F). He tried to shout for help, but soon drifted in and out of consciousness.

For the next 15 minutes, cabin crew struggled unsuccessfully to pull Lancaster back inside the plane and to comfort passengers who believed they were in mortal danger. Copilot Atchison knew he had to lose height at once, before Lancaster suffocated in the thin air. He was almost certain that the pilot was already dead since his body was now covered in a thin film of frost. He looked so contorted as he flapped around the cabin window, that the crew thought he must have broken his back.

The nearest airport was Southampton and permission for an emergency landing was quickly secured. As two crew members clung desperately to Lancaster's legs, Atchinson executed a perfect landing.

The plane was swiftly surrounded by airport firecrew, who were amazed to see Lancaster lift his head and ask what had happened. The pilot they all thought was dead had suffered only a touch of frostbite and minor fractures to his arms.

Vulovic's record breaking fall

Yugoslavian stewardess Vesna Vulovic busied herself in the rear galley of the plane, tidying meal trays for her handful of passengers, in the early evening of January 27, 1972.

It had been a quiet flight. The DC-9, flying from Stockholm to Belgrade, was only a quarter full. The crew had heard that Yugoslav Prime Minister Dzemal Bijedic would be on the plane, but he had not boarded.

As they flew 10,000m (33,000ft) above the East German-Czechoslovakian border, Vulovic stared nonchalantly out of a window, hoping to catch a glimpse of the moonlit Erzgebirge mountains. But as she did so, a bomb planted by Croatian terrorists intending to assassinate Bijedic, detonated.

In the tail of the plane, Vulovic watched in horror as a terrible explosion ripped through the aircraft. The tail section broke away and began to plummet inexorably to the ground. As she spun around the freezing night sky she knew her life was over and awaited the hideous blow that would end it. But instead of a thud, there was a huge splash. The tail had landed in a deep pond at Serbska Kamenice, in Czechoslovakia.

Vulovic remembered very little after that, except regaining consciousness and talking to a doctor who had rushed to the disaster. She was gravely injured, but unlike everyone else on the flight, she had survived. To this day, no one else has fallen from a greater height and lived.

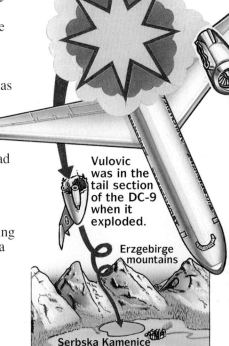

Vulovic was in the tail section of the DC-9 when it exploded.

Erzgebirge mountains

Serbska Kamenice

Wolff to the rescue

The news that filtered back to London in the summer of 1843 was disturbing. Two British army officers, named Conolly and Stoddard, were being held prisoner in the city of Bukhara, in central Asia.

Their captor was Emir* Nasrullah Khan. He was known to be extremely hostile to foreigners and his reputation for wanton cruelty had reached even Britain, 8,000km (5,000 miles) away.

The two officers had been tortured and thrown into a pit full of deadly snakes and insects. Whether they were still alive was unclear.

Joseph Wolff. Born in Bavaria, he settled in England after 20 years of travel as a missionary.

Marauding gangs

Bukhara nestled on the edge of inhospitable desert terrain, where marauding bandit gangs plagued any visitor unfortunate enough to cross their path. In the 1840s only a handful of intrepid Europeans had ever dared to go there.

Many people in London felt that if Conolly and Stoddard were still alive, then someone ought try to rescue them. But the British Government was not prepared to send anyone on such a hazardous mission.

Bavarian Wolff

The plight of the two soldiers soon reached the ears of a country parson who was visiting friends in London. He was 52, Bavarian, magnificently overweight and, some thought, quite mad. His name was Joseph Wolff.

Apart from Conolly and Stoddard, Wolff was the only man in England who had been to Bukhara. He had visited as a missionary, 10 years before. He spoke the language and

Nasrullah Khan, Emir of Bukhara. Despite his cruel reputation he was a shrewd and incorruptible ruler.

was familiar with local custom.

Over the years, the British Army had rescued him from certain death several times and he felt he owed them a great debt. A rescue mission to Bukhara would be one way of repaying it.

So he placed a letter in the *Morning Herald* newspaper seeking money for an expedition. This brought in sufficient funds and an offer from the P & O shipping line of free travel as far as Turkey.

Before he settled into his life as a country parson, Wolff had spent two decades working as a missionary in Asia and Africa, where he had acquired a reputation as a born survivor. Attacked and robbed from Bukhara to Timbuktu, he had endured a succession of extraordinary misfortunes. On one occasion he was tied to a horse's tail by slave traders and dragged across the desert. On another, bandits stole all his clothes, leaving him to cross the snowy Hindu Kush mountains stark naked. After that, the dysentery, cholera, earthquakes and shipwrecks he endured were minor irritations.

It was not just physical resilience that kept him alive; he also had personal qualities that were indispensable. Unlike some European visitors, he had a healthy respect for the cultures he visited and an uncanny ability to make influential friends.

Grand Dervish

Wolff's plan to rescue Conolly and Stoddard was simple, and typical of his tremendous daring. He would march into Bukhara with as much pomp and ceremony as he could muster and ask the notorious Emir to release the two officers. Supposing that the more important he looked and sounded, the more reluctant the Emir would be to harm him, Wolff packed his finest clerical clothing and invented a title for himself: "Grand Dervish* of

*Dervish is an Arabic word for holy man.

England, Scotland and Ireland, and the whole of Europe and America". He also took 24 Bibles, a collection of maps, 36 silver watches and 36 copies of *Robinson Crusoe*, translated into Arabic. Wolff knew the value of a good bribe in a tight situation. Silver watches were always a source of great interest and *Robinson Crusoe*, he was sure was the sort of book anyone would be eager to read.

Bukhara bound

So, with no official support or authority from the British Government, Wolff set sail from Southampton for Constantinople (now Istanbul) in October, 1843.

During an idle moment, Wolff glanced through the ship's visitors' book, where distinguished passengers recorded their names. A shiver of foreboding ran through him as he came across the signature of Arthur Conolly, who had taken the very same boat on his way to Bukhara, several years previously.

At Constantinople, Wolff persuaded the Sultan* and the highest ranking Islamic officials to provide him with letters of introduction. These

The trip from Southampton to Bukhara – by steamship, horse and foot – took 28 weeks.

might convince the chieftains and governors he met on his travels that he was well connected, and maybe they would be more likely to help rather than harm him.

Trip to Tehran

Wolff recruited guides and servants in Constantinople and, making his way on foot and horseback, he pressed on to Tehran, the capital of Persia (now called Iran).

Here, British Ambassador Justin Sheil tried to persuade Wolff to abandon his mission. Sheil was certain Conolly and Stoddard had been executed, and believed anyone sent to investigate their deaths would be killed too.

Wolff had come to the same conclusion, but felt obliged to continue. He wrote that if he returned home without going to Bukhara, then everyone would say that his expedition "had been a piece of humbug and was the work of a braggart."

While he was in Tehran, Sheil introduced Wolff to the Shah (King) of Persia. The Shah took a liking to the portly Bavarian and wrote to the Emir asking him to treat Wolff as a respected visitor.

Desert escort

Between Tehran and Bukhara lay 1,000km (600 miles) of harsh desert terrain, populated

by slave traders and bandits. Fortunately, in Meshed, near the Persian border, Wolff acquired another useful ally – the local governor. He warned Wolff of the dangers ahead, and provided him with nine armed guards.

But as the rock and rubble of the desert gradually changed to the green pastures of Bukhara, his escort grew fearful, and one by one they began to slip away. Wolff marched on at the head of his dwindling party, reading aloud from the Bible, as if to ward off the evil he felt closing in on him.

The sight of a huge fat man, resplendent in his scarlet silk hood and fine clerical uniform soon attracted much attention. By the time Wolff arrived at the city gates on April 27, huge crowds had turned out to see him.

Grand arrival

A visitor arriving in such a flamboyant style as this could not fail to secure an audience with the Emir. Besides, Wolff also had letters from sultans, shahs and ambassadors, beseeching Nasrullah Khan to see him. He was brought to a grand palace and ushered through cool marble corridors into a crowded court room. At one end, surrounded by fawning advisors, sat the Emir. Clothed in plain cottons, distant and withdrawn, he was as still and

Wolff's journey

England
EUROPE
Constantinople
AFRICA
Bukhara

Black Sea
Caspian Sea
Aral Sea
Constantinople (now Istanbul)
Tehran
Meshed
Bukhara

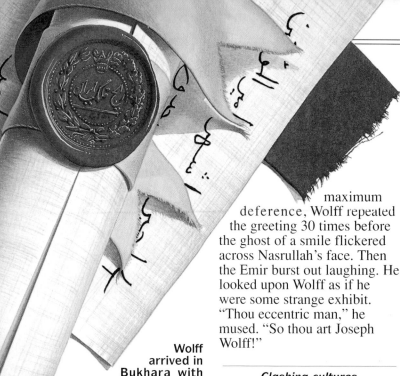

Wolff arrived in Bukhara with letters of introduction from eminent Islamic rulers.

silent as a statue. On top of his head perched a neat silk turban, and much of his face was covered by a black, bushy beard. His dark eyes were the only part of him that mōved, and they turned a venomous gaze on the strange man who approached him.

Maximum manners

Wolff was well versed in the correct way to behave at such meetings. He knew it was necessary to show an almost religious reverence to the ruler. He stood before the inscrutable Emir and recited the customary greeting of his court, "Refuge of the World, Peace to the King," which any visitor was required to say three times, while stroking his own beard (another mark of respect).

Keen to show maximum deference, Wolff repeated the greeting 30 times before the ghost of a smile flickered across Nasrullah's face. Then the Emir burst out laughing. He looked upon Wolff as if he were some strange exhibit. "Thou eccentric man," he mused. "So thou art Joseph Wolff!"

Clashing cultures

Wolff immediately asked what had happened to Conolly and Stoddard, and was abruptly told they had been executed. Conolly, explained the Emir, "had a long nose" (meaning he was arrogant), and Stoddard "had not paid him the proper respect".

It soon became clear that there was more to it than that. Aside from the two officers' haughty European superiority, the Emir was sure that both men had been involved in a plot to overthrow him.

The society Wolff found

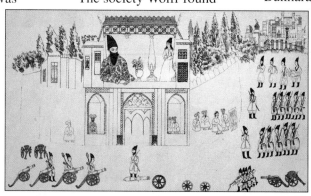

Contemporary engraving of Bukhara. This is the house of Abdul Samut Khan, one of the Emir's principal advisors, and Wolff's greatest enemy.

himself in was one of curious contradictions. The Emir was undoubtedly cruel and tyrannous, and had the most extraordinary temper, but even the poorest of his subjects were permitted to approach him for advice or judgment. He was honest, and could not be bribed. He seemed genuinely astonished that Wolff had come all this way just to enquire about the fate of two British officers, and seemed concerned that the situation had caused ill feeling in Britain.

Wolff was given an apartment in the palace and for a few weeks he remained as the Emir's guest. Nasrullah Khan was eager to learn about his visitor and the far away country he represented. He was fascinated to hear about steamships and locomotives, and curious to know whether there was witchcraft in Britain, and why Queen Victoria did not execute more of her subjects.

Terror and treachery

But the longer Wolff stayed in this exotic and unfamiliar court, the more uncomfortable he became, especially when he was taken to Conolly and Stoddard's place of execution and shown their heads.

Soon after he arrived in Bukhara he was befriended by one of the Emir's principal advisers, Abdul Samut Khan, known as the Naib. This man told him how hard he had worked to save the lives of the two British officers. He seemed like a useful ally, but the price of his friendship was money. When Wolff's funds ran out, four weeks into his stay, the Naib turned against him, and boasted that it was he, after all, who had persuaded the Emir to kill Conolly and Stoddard.

Lost gamble

Although Wolff's requests to leave were always granted, whenever the date of departure arrived he was forbidden to go. The Emir and Naib amused themselves with his increasing discomfort, and began to taunt him openly. When Wolff requested the remains of Conolly and Stoddard to take home, the Emir told him that the only bones that would be returning to England would be his own.

Wolff realized that patience was not going to win him this particular battle, and attempted to escape. He failed, and was placed under house arrest.

His fate looked grim. The Emir departed to a distant province on a campaign to subdue a rebellion against him and while he was away, the Naib began to suggest openly to court advisors that Wolff be executed.

Wolff tried hard not to be seen to be intimidated. Confined indoors throughout the steamy summer, he attempted to cheer himself up by singing German romantic songs at the top of his voice.

Court intrigue

Although he was a prisoner, and constantly watched, he was still allowed to have visitors. He had made friends among the small Jewish community in Bukhara, and they called on him regularly. They conversed in Hebrew, a language Wolff's guards did not understand and, pretending to read aloud to each other from the Bible, they were able to speak freely of the latest talk concerning his fate.

But one morning, an Islamic holy man visited and demanded that Wolff renounce his Christianity and become a Muslim. Enraged, Wolff drove him from the room with an angry bellow. He began to fear that death was only days away.

His next visitor was the Bukharan executioner who had put to death Conolly and Stoddard. The man explained he had come to inspect him, so he could best judge how to kill him. Wolff was overcome. Despite his audacity he was not a brave man and faced his fate with icy dread.

Final message

He prayed fervently and wrote a last message in his Bible to his loved ones. "My dearest Georgiana and Henry, I have loved both of you unto death, Your affectionate husband and father, J.Wolff." And then he waited, left alone with his fear. The thought of the executioners blade slitting his poor throat filled him with a livid terror.

The hours dragged by, then footsteps approached. The door flew open and Wolff was dragged from his room.

Behind the scenes

But it was to the Emir's palace, rather than the execution ground that he was taken. Behind the scenes Wolff's strategy of enlisting the support of anyone who might prove useful had paid off. The Shah of Persia, hearing of his plight, had sent an ambassador, Abbas Kouli Khan, to plead for his release. Fortunately for Wolff, Nasrullah's campaign to

subdue his rebellious province had gone badly. He returned to Bukhara feeling vulnerable, and certainly not strong enough to antagonize the Shah, who was the most powerful ruler in the area. Executing Wolff was not worth the trouble it would cause. The Emir summoned the Persian ambassador and told him "I make a present to you of Joseph Wolff."

Showered with gifts

Wolff was brought before Nasrullah Khan and showered with money and gifts. The Emir asked that Wolff return home with a Bukharan ambassador, and stated that he wished to be on good terms with England. Dazed by his good fortune, Wolff prepared to depart. His life, which had hung by a very slender thread, was now spared.

On August 3, 1844, the people of Bukhara once again turned out in their thousands to see Joseph Wolff. He had arrived almost alone, reading from his Bible. He left in a splendid, noisy procession of ambassadors, merchants, holy men and 2,000 camels.

Wolff was given a horse, a shawl and 90 tillahs (Bukharan gold coins) as compensation for his imprisonment.

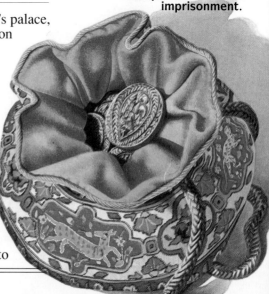

Ted cheats death on sinking Hood

In the chilly waters of the North Atlantic, just below the perpetual ice field of the Arctic Ocean, a grey May dawn broke before 2:00am. Pitching through a rolling grey sea, scything wind and flurries of snow, a great grey battleship headed relentlessly toward its prey. The year was 1941.

The ship was *HMS Hood* – the most celebrated vessel in the British Navy. The 1,421 men on board had been ready for battle throughout the night. Most were finding it was impossible to sleep, for they were about to engage in a life or death struggle with two of Germany's mightiest warships – *Bismarck* and *Prinz Eugen*.

Platform perch

High above the deck, in the dimly lit compass platform, sat Vice-Admiral Lancelot Holland. Surrounded by his chief lieutenants – the ship's captain, and navigation, signal and gunnery officers – Holland scoured the horizon, his fingers tapping anxiously on his binoculars.

Signalman Ted Briggs in 1941.

Waiting on the *Hood*'s masters in this lofty perch was 18-year-old signalman Ted Briggs, whose task it was to carry messages to other parts of the ship. Briggs had first set eyes on the *Hood* on a trip to the Yorkshire coast in 1935, when he was 12. It was love at first sight, and he had decided then and there to join the Navy to sail on her. Now, six years later, here he was, watching the calm deliberations of her senior officers with a mixture of fear and fascination.

Compass platform

The *Bismarck*. The striped camouflage was intended to make the ship look smaller.

The ship's emblem was the crest of statesman Count von Bismarck.

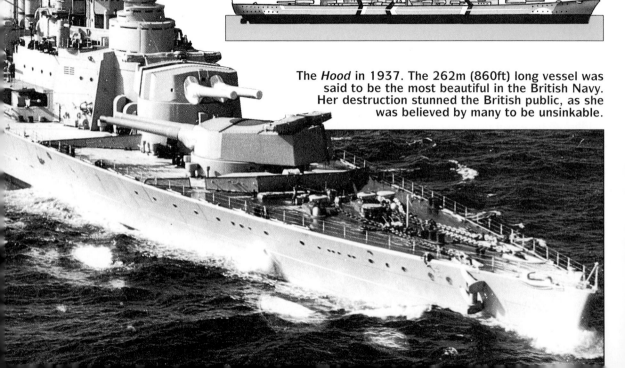

The *Hood* in 1937. The 262m (860ft) long vessel was said to be the most beautiful in the British Navy. Her destruction stunned the British public, as she was believed by many to be unsinkable.

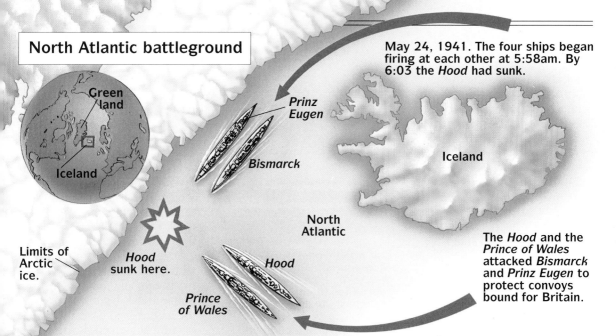

North Atlantic battleground

May 24, 1941. The four ships began firing at each other at 5:58am. By 6:03 the *Hood* had sunk.

Greenland

Iceland

Prinz Eugen

Bismarck

Iceland

North Atlantic

Limits of Arctic ice.

Hood sunk here.

Hood

Prince of Wales

The *Hood* and the *Prince of Wales* attacked *Bismarck* and *Prinz Eugen* to protect convoys bound for Britain.

Fighting novice

The *Hood* had never before had to fight another ship. Briggs knew it would be a bloody business, but he was confident that his beloved *Hood*, and the battleship *Prince of Wales*, which was sailing alongside her, would soon dispatch any ship that crossed their path.

But Briggs was mistaken. *Bismarck* was an opponent no one would have wished for. Heavily armed and well protected, the aggressive angles and sweep of the ship made a striking contrast with the stately elegance of the *Hood*.

Like the *Hood*, she was over 0.25km (1/6 mile) long, but she was also 20 years younger and the very model of modern naval technology. Compared to the *Bismarck*, the *Hood* looked positively antiquated.

Battle begins

The two German ships were sighted at 5:35am. Ominous black dots 27km (17 miles) away, they would soon be within range of the *Hood*'s huge guns.

At 20km (13 miles) the *Hood* opened fire, her shells hurling toward *Bismarck* and *Prinz Eugen* at over twice the speed of sound. Nearly half a minute passed before huge plumes of water, as high as tower blocks, rose around the two approaching ships. The *Hood* had missed.

Terrified anticipation

Up on the compass platform, Briggs watched the *Bismarck*'s retort. Gold flashes with red cores winked from the distant ship. A low whine built to a howling crescendo as the shells made a 20 second journey between the two ships.

The *Hood's* emblem – a crow holding an anchor. This symbol was found on everything from engine room controls to the ship's stationery.

Briggs' terrified anticipation ended when four huge columns of foam erupted to the right of the ship. Then an explosion knocked him off his feet.

The *Hood* had been hit at the base of its mainmast and fire spread rapidly. On deck, anti-aircraft shells exploded like firecrackers. On the platform, the screams of wounded men trickled from the voice-pipes* that kept the ship's commanders in touch with their vessel.

Fatal blow

As the *Hood* turned to give its gunners a better view of the approaching enemy, another huge explosion rocked the ship, and Briggs was again thrown off his feet. A shell from *Bismarck* had penetrated deep within the hull and detonated her main ammunition supplies.

Aboard the *Prince of Wales* men saw an eerily silent explosion – like a huge red tongue – shoot four times the height of the ship. Pieces of the mainmast, a huge crane and part of a gun turret flew through the air.

When Briggs got up he felt in mortal fear for his life and knew instinctively that his ship had been fatally damaged. The *Hood* listed slowly to the right and the helmsman shouted through the voice-pipe that the ship's steering had failed.

To Briggs' relief the *Hood* rolled slowly back to level, but this relief was short-lived. The

The *Hood* from *Prince of Wales*. Moments after this photograph was taken a huge explosion four times the height of the mainmast would sink the ship.

ship lurched to the left and began to roll over. There was no order to abandon ship. As the floor became steeper and steeper the crew on the compass platform headed unprompted to the exit ladder. An officer stood aside to let Briggs go first. Slumped in his chair, Vice-Admiral

Lancelot Holland sat stunned and defeated.

The Hood sinks

Briggs climbed down a ladder to a lower deck on the tilting ship, but the sea was already gushing around his legs. With desperate haste he began to discard any clothing that would weigh him down, managing to lose his steel helmet and gas mask before being sucked into the icy water.

Dragged deep beneath the ship he felt an intense pressure in his ears and thought he was going to die. Unable to reach the surface and desperate to breathe he gulped down mouthfuls of water. As he was drowning, panic subsided. A childlike, blissful security swept over him, and Briggs thought of his mother tucking him into bed. But his peaceful resignation was interrupted. A great surge of water suddenly shot him to the surface.

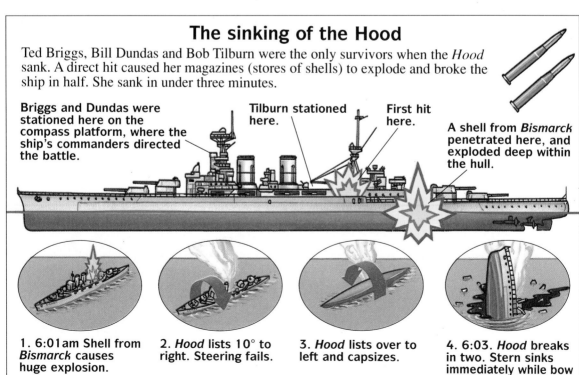

The sinking of the Hood

Ted Briggs, Bill Dundas and Bob Tilburn were the only survivors when the *Hood* sank. A direct hit caused her magazines (stores of shells) to explode and broke the ship in half. She sank in under three minutes.

Briggs and Dundas were stationed here on the compass platform, where the ship's commanders directed the battle.

Tilburn stationed here.

First hit here.

A shell from *Bismarck* penetrated here, and exploded deep within the hull.

1. 6:01am Shell from *Bismarck* causes huge explosion.

2. *Hood* lists 10° to right. Steering fails.

3. *Hood* lists over to left and capsizes.

4. 6:03. *Hood* breaks in two. Stern sinks immediately while bow points toward the sky.

Choking and spluttering, Briggs gasped down great lungfuls of air, and took in a scene of unimaginable horror. All around were blazing pools of oil. What remained of the *Hood* was 45m (150ft) away. Her bows were vertical in the sea, the dislocated guns in her forward turrets were disappearing fast into the water. She was making a horrific hissing sound as white-hot metal and bubbling, blistering paint and wood made contact with the icy water. The *Prince of Wales* sailed close by, nearly colliding with the wreckage. The bow of the Hood towered over her like a nightmarish spire.

When the ship's radio wiring came down on him, Bob Tilburn had to cut himself free.

Briggs escapes

Realizing he was close enough to be sucked down again by the whirlpool currents the huge sinking ship was making, Briggs swam away through the oily sea as hard as he could. All around were dozens of small wooden rafts which had floated away when the *Hood* capsized, and he hauled himself onto one.

Looking back, nothing remained of the ship except a small patch of blazing oil where the bow had disappeared. It was a mere three minutes since the *Bismarck*'s guns had found their target.

Briggs was still in terrible danger. Shells from *Bismarck* and *Prinz Eugen* were falling around the *Prince of Wales*, only yards away, and the oil that surrounded him could ignite at any moment.

Other survivors

As he paddled away from the oil, he looked for other survivors. Two were close by. All three paddled toward one another and held their rafts together by linking arms.

On one raft was Midshipman (junior officer) Bill Dundas, who had been on the compass platform with Briggs. When the *Hood* capsized he kicked his way out of a window and swam away from the ship.

The other man was Able Seaman Bob Tilburn, who had been manning a gun position at the side of the ship. His had been the luckiest escape. He had survived exploding ammunition lockers and had been showered with falling debris and the bodies of men from the decks above. When the *Hood* capsized, he jumped into the water only to have the ship come down on top of him. Radio wiring had wrapped itself around his seaboots and he had cut himself free with a knife.

The three men were now in danger of freezing to death. To stop them from falling asleep and dying of exposure Dundas made them sing *Roll out the barrel* – a wartime pop song.

Fortunately they did not have to wait too long for help to arrive. The British destroyer *Electra* had spotted the three men and was heading toward them.

Ted Briggs was too cold to haul himself up to the ship and had to be lifted aboard. In *Electra*'s sick bay, frozen clothes were cut from his body and he was given rum to warm him up.

The *Electra* and three other ships had been sent to look for survivors. There was so little sign of life when they arrived at the scene of the sinking that they thought they must have gone off course. Briggs, Dundas and Tilburn, and a few wooden rafts, were all that was left. The *Hood* had taken the rest of her 1,421 crew – Vice-Admiral to engine room stoker – to the bottom of the North Atlantic.

Ted Briggs with his mother and sister, a week after the *Hood* went down. Mrs Briggs received a telegram telling her he was safe only an hour after radio reports announced that the *Hood* had sunk with little chance of survivors.

Surviving for yourself

Many survival skills can be easily learned. Following a disaster, the techniques shown here could make the difference between life and death.

Help signals

One of the most vital skills a survivor can have is knowing how to signal for help. Making three fires, or three columns of smoke, for example, are help signals which are recognized throughout the world.

Smoke from a signal fire can be made to contrast with the surrounding environment.

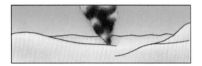

In deserts, rubber can be burned to create thick, black smoke.

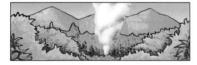

In jungles, green leaves can be used to create white smoke.

Six blasts or flashes from a whistle, mirror or flashlight, at one minute intervals, is also a way of calling for help. If you do not have a mirror, use a belt buckle, polished cup or anything else that reflects the Sun's rays. These flashes can be seen up to 100km (60 miles) away. In deserts, flashes have been seen at distances of up to 160km (100 miles).

Morse code

Morse code is a signal system where each letter of the alphabet is represented by a sequence of dots (short signals) and dashes (longer signals). Mirrors, flashlights or whistles are three ways in which you can transmit it.

The emergency help signal in Morse code is SOS. Many people think this stands for "Save Our Souls", but these letters were chosen because S and O are the two easiest letters to remember in Morse. S is three dots . . . O is three dashes - - - . To do this signal with a flashlight you would need to make three quick flashes, followed by three longer flashes, then another three quick flashes.

Other signals

The letters SOS can also be written on the ground. The best place for this is on high ground, or in a clearing. You can use stones or branches. Make the letters as big as possible, so they can be seen from the air. This works especially well if the letters are large enough to make shadows, which makes them stand out even better.

Extreme heat

In very hot conditions you may suffer from heatstroke. This causes fever, and can lead to convulsions and coma. It may even be fatal. Survivors stranded in hot surroundings can take these precautions:
• Drink as much water as you can. In high temperatures your body may need four times as much water as usual.
• If your supply of water is low, only use it to moisten your mouth. You can also suck a small pebble

Cardboard mask

as this stimulates saliva glands in your mouth and relieves thirst. Chewing on grass will also provide a little moisture.
• Shelter from the Sun during the day. Travel only at night.
• Keep clothes on – this helps prevent sunburn and water loss, as sweat evaporates more slowly from your skin.
• Keep your head covered at all times. If you do not have a hat, wrap a loose-fitting cloth around your head.
• You can make a simple mask to cut down on glare from bright sunlight. Use available materials, such as cardboard and elastic bands.

Making fire

To start a fire, you need three basic materials, called tinder, kindling and fuel. If you do not have matches to light your fire, you could use a glass lens to focus the Sun's rays, or chip a flint stone against steel, to make sparks.

Tinder
This is quite easy to ignite and will set fire to kindling.

Kindling
This increases the temperature enough to set fire to fuel.

Fuel
This generates heat for warmth and cooking, and smoke for signals.

Extreme cold

One of the survivor's greatest enemies is cold – even deserts are cold at night. If your body temperature drops more than a couple of degrees you may suffer from hypothermia. This causes drowsiness and disorientation, and can be fatal. Extreme cold may also freeze your flesh, causing a condition known as frostbite. Follow these steps to prevent frostbite and hypothermia:
• Keep dry. When you are wet, you become even colder as water evaporates from clothes.
• If you have been out in snow, brush it off when returning to shelter. Otherwise it will melt and soak your clothing.
• Wrinkle your face, and wriggle your fingers and toes at regular intervals. This keeps blood circulating in the extremities of your body.
• Do not wear tight clothing. This restricts circulation. With looser clothes, an insulating layer of air keeps out cold.
• Wear as many clothes as possible. A layer of dry leaves or moss stuffed between two pairs of socks will also help insulate your feet. (Be careful not to stuff them too tight.)

Snow shelter

A shelter is essential in cold conditions. The diagram on the right shows how survivors trapped in a snowy forest can make themselves a snow shelter using a large blanket.

Fill blanket with leaves and sticks, to make a semicircular structure. Shape snow over blanket and allow to harden.

Pull out contents of sack. Door can be made with small bag filled with sticks. Insulate floor with leaves and twigs.

Air hole
Door

Thirst

Without food, you could live for a month. Without water you may die after three days. If you are stranded with little water, take these precautions:
• In high temperatures, take shelter or wear protective clothing. You can sweat as much as 4 litres (7 pints) of water in an hour.
• In cold conditions, always breathe through your nose rather than your mouth. This warms air entering your lungs. You lose water in your breath, especially if the air you inhale is cold.
• Eat as little as possible. When you digest food your body uses a lot of water.
• Do as little exercise as you can, as this makes you sweat.
• Do not drink sea water. This has a high salt content and will make you even more thirsty*.

Finding water

At sea, collect as much rain as possible. In a desert, plants and animals indicate that water is nearby. An area with some vegetation will be a good place to build a solar still – a device for extracting water from the air and soil.

A still like the one below will also collect water from the dew that falls at dawn.

Sun heats interior and water within sand evaporates. Droplets form on sheet and run into container.

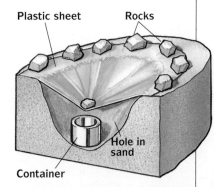

Plastic sheet   Rocks

Hole in sand
Container

---

*This is disputed. See p. 46.

After the ordeal

Apollo 13

(Space catastrophe for unlucky 13, p.28-32)

One American newspaper remarked of *Apollo 13*'s close escape "Never in recorded history has a journey of such peril been watched and waited-out by almost the entire human race." The three astronauts arrived back at their home town of Houston, Texas, to find US president Richard Nixon waiting to greet them. None returned to space again.

James Lovell retired from NASA in 1973 to work for the Centel Corporation in Chicago. **Fred Haise** was at the controls of the first Space Shuttle *Enterprise* when it made its maiden Earth flight in 1977. **Jack Swigert** took up a career in politics. He was elected to public office in Colorado in November, 1982, but died a month later of bone cancer.

William Bligh

("Breadfruit" Bligh's boatload of trouble, p.13-17)

Bligh returned to his family in England to discover that he was the father of twin girls and to write a best selling account of the *Bounty* mutiny. In the summer of 1790, he faced a court-martial for the loss of his ship, but was acquitted.

The following year he was given a new ship, *HMS Providence*, returned to Tahiti, and successfully transported breadfruit plants to the West Indies, where they still grow to this day.

In 1808, he was appointed Governor of New South Wales, Australia. His attempts to restrict the import of alcohol to

the territory led to an army mutiny against him, and he was imprisoned by his own troops for 26 months. This did not harm his Navy career. By the time he retired he had reached the rank of rear admiral. He died at 63, in 1817.

Fletcher Christian, who led the *Bounty* mutiny, fled with nine other mutineers and 18 Tahitians to remote and uninhabited Pitcairn Island, in the South Pacific. Here, Christian and most of his companions met violent deaths, squabbling among themselves or with the Tahitians.

Today, the island is inhabited by 18 families. Between them they have only four surnames, three of which – Christian, Young and Brown – belong to the original mutineers.

This 1808 engraving depicts Bligh attempting to evade mutinous troops in Australia.

Alain Bombard

(Plenty of fish in sea, says scientist, p.46-49)

Alain Bombard returned to France to write an account of his voyage across the Atlantic – *The Bombard Story**. He also founded a marine research laboratory at St. Malo, France. His boat *L'Hérétique* found a home in the French Navy Museum in Paris. Today, he is a familiar face on French television, where he is well known as an environmental campaigner.

Ted Briggs

(Ted cheats death on sinking Hood, p.56-59)

Ted Briggs survived the war. Serving for 35 years in the British Royal Navy, he rose to the rank of lieutenant, and was awarded the MBE (Member of the British Empire) by the British Government. He now lives in Hampshire, England, and is a prominent member of the Hood Association – an organization set up to preserve the memory of his former ship.

The Hindenburg

(Hindenburg's hydrogen hell, p.9-12)

In Germany, the ruling Nazi regime saw the *Hindenburg* as a symbol of their power and prestige. They were quick to blame the disaster on sabotage, but could produce no serious evidence to back this up. Hugo Eckener, chairman of the Zeppelin Reederei, described the fire as "the hopeless end of a great dream". The notion of huge airships carrying passengers across the oceans died in the flames at Lakehurst. To this day, airships remain an airborne gimmick, suitable mainly for advertising slogans.

Evel Knievel

(Death or glory for "Last Gladiator", p.36-37)

The Snake River jump was such a financially successful "retirement", Knievel could not resist the lure of further stunts, including a motorbike leap over 13 buses at Wembley Stadium, London, in 1976. These earned him an alleged $65 million (£43 million)

 *See Further reading p. 64.

fortune, and an entry in the *Guinness Book of Records* for the greatest number of broken bones (433 in total).

Following a baseball bat attack on a journalist who had written an uncomplimentary autobiography, he spent five months in prison. Currently claiming to be broke ("I don't own so much as a block of wood now," he was reported as saying in 1994), he makes a living selling his own paintings and managing his stunt rider son Robbie.

Pu'u O'o

(Film crew in lava inferno, p.43-45)

The film *Sliver* was completed without any shots of smoking volcanoes. One leading character in the film does confess, however, to a great fascination in volcanoes, and admits he has fantasies about flying into one. **Don Shearer** and **Tom Hauptman**, who flew rescue helicopters into Pu'u O'o, are both thanked in the film's credits.

Susie Rijnhart

(Susie Rijnhart's Tibetan trek, p.18-21)

After reaching safe territory in China, Rijnhart made her way back to Canada. Several years later she remarried and returned to Tibet with her husband, intent on further missionary work. She died in childbirth three weeks after crossing into Tibet from China.

Saint-Exupéry

(Mirage misery for Saint-Exupéry, p.22-25)

Following his desert rescue, Saint-Ex spent the remainder of his life continuing to enhance his reputation as both a writer

and a pioneer aviator. His experiences in the Sahara are recounted in his book *Terre des hommes** (*Wind, Sand and Stars*) published in 1939. His most famous book, the fable *Le Petit Prince* (*The Little Prince*) was published in 1943.

During World War Two he served in the French Air Force, and fled to New York when France surrendered. Returning to serve with the Free French Forces in North Africa, he was shot down and killed during a reconnaissance flight over Corsica. He was 44. After his death the French government awarded him the Commandeur de la Légion d'Honneur medal.

Ernest Shackleton

(Marooned in a polar wilderness, p.38-42)

The survivors of Shackleton's Antarctic expedition returned to a Europe ensnared in World War One. Almost all volunteered for the armed services and two, a junior officer and a seaman, were killed in action. Shackleton, his deputy **Frank Wild** and *Endurance*'s captain **Frank Worsley** were sent to the North Russian front, where their knowledge of polar conditions would be useful. Many of *Endurance*'s crew served in minesweepers.

In 1921, Shackleton returned to the Antarctic with many of his *Endurance* shipmates, intent on further exploration. He died of a heart attack at Grytviken, South Georgia, in January, 1922, and is buried on the island.

Joe Simpson

(Simpson's icy tomb, p.33-35)

Following his reunion with Simon Yates, Simpson endured a six day wait before receiving

medical attention for his injured leg. Back home in Britain, Doctors warned him he would never climb again. Defying medical opinion he made an extraordinary recovery and now climbs all over the world. In 1992, he returned to Peru and climbed six mountains in three weeks. He now divides his time between mountaineering, writing and working as a guide for a trekking company. His account of his mishap on Siula Grande, *Touching The Void**, has sold 500,000 copies and been translated into 14 languages.

Squalus

(Dive to disaster, p.4-8)

Squalus was salvaged six months after its disastrous crash-dive. Renamed *Sailfish* (navies traditionally rename all salvaged ships), she fought in World War Two. On December 4, 1943, she sank the Japanese aircraft carrier *Chuyo*. By an extraordinary coincidence, among the survivors were members of the submarine *Sculpin*, which had assisted in the rescue of the *Squalus*. They had been taken prisoner when their submarine was sunk and *Chuyo* had been ferrying them into captivity.

Joseph Wolff

(Wolff to the rescue, p.52-55)

It took Wolff nine months to travel from Bukhara back to England. He finally arrived home in April, 1845.

Promising his family he would never travel abroad again, he spent the rest of his days as vicar of the quiet country parish of Ile Brewers in Somerset, where his eccentric manner continued to bemuse all those who knew him. He died in 1862, aged 67.

Further reading

If you would like to know more about some of these stories, the following books contain useful information.

Apollo Expeditions to the Moon edited by Edgar Cortright (NASA, 1980). Contains James Lovell's account of the *Apollo 13* disaster: *"Houston, We've had a Problem"*.
The Bombard Story by Alain Bombard (André Deutsch, 1953)
Captain Bligh and Mr. Christian by Richard Hough (Cassell Ltd., 1979)
Endurance – Shackleton's Incredible Voyage by Alfred Lansing (Hodder & Stoughton, 1959)
Few Survived – A Comprehensive Survey of Submarine Accidents and Disasters by Edwyn Gray (Leo Cooper, 1986)
Flagship Hood by Alan Coles and Ted Briggs (Robert Hale Ltd., 1985)
The Giant Airships by Douglas Botting (Time-Life Books, 1981)
Improve Your Survival Skills by Lucy Smith (Usborne Publishing, 1987)
A Mission to Bokhara by Joseph Wolff (Routledge and Kegan Paul, 1969 – Facsimile of original 1852 edition)
Touching the Void by Joe Simpson (Jonathan Cape, Ltd., 1988)
Wind, Sand and Stars by Antoine de Saint-Exupéry (William Heinemann, 1939)
With the Tibetans in Tent and Temple by Susie Carson Rijnhart (Oliphant, Anderson & Ferrier, 1901)

Acknowledgements and photo credits

The Publishers would like to thank the following for their help and advice:

John Barry, Llanrwst; Ted Briggs, Fareham; Clive Bunyan, Science Museum, London; Dr. David Killingray, Reader in History, Goldsmiths College, University of London; Iain MacKenzie, Maritime Information Centre, National Maritime Museum, London; Doug Millard, Associate Curator for Space Technology, Science Museum, London; Raja Rahawani Raja Mamat and Norhashimi Saad, Coventry; Joe Simpson, Sheffield.

The publishers would also like to thank the following for permission to reproduce their photographs in this book: Associated Press, London (45); Bilderdienst Süddeutscher Verlag, Munich (10 bottom right); Ted Briggs, Fareham, UK (3, 56 top, 59); Ray Delány/Perpetual Unit Trust, UK (33); e.t. archive/National Maritime Museum, London (13 bottom); Hulton-Deutsch, London (38 bottom, 52); Imperial War Museum, London (58); NASA, Houston, USA (28, 31, 32); National Archives, Washington, USA (4, 5, 6, 8); Popperfoto, Overstone, UK (10-11, 56 bottom); Press Association, London (51); Roger-Viollet, Paris (46); Roger-Viollet © Collection Viollet (22, 25); Royal Geographical Society, London (38 top, 39); Frank Spooner Pictures, London/Gamma/David Burdett (36, 37); Topham Picture Source, Edenbridge, UK (11 right, 42); Ullstein Bilderdienst, Berlin (9, 10 bottom left, 12).

Picture Researcher: Diana Morris.

Every effort has been made to trace the copyright holders of material in this book. If any rights have been omitted, the publishers offer to rectify this in any subsequent editions following notification.

Index

First published in Great Britain in 1995 by Usborne Publishing Ltd.

ISBN 0-439-35329-7